Microprocessor System
Development

Microprocessor System Development

Alain Amghar

Translated from the French by

John C. C. Nelson

Department of Electrical and Electronic Engineering
University of Leeds

Masson

Prentice Hall

First published in French by Masson, Paris, under the title
Méthodes de développement d'un système à microprocesseurs by
Alain Amghar

© Masson, Paris, 1989

This edition first published in English by
Prentice Hall International and Masson

Prentice Hall International (UK) Ltd
66 Wood Lane End, Hemel Hempstead
Hertfordshire HP2 4RG
A division of
Simon & Schuster International Group

© Prentice Hall International (UK) Ltd and Masson, Paris, 1990

Typeset in 10/12 pt Times
by Keyset Composition, Colchester

Printed and bound in Great Britain
by Dotesios Printers Ltd, Trowbridge, Wiltshire.

Library of Congress Cataloging-in-Publication Data

Amghar, Alain.
  [Méthodes de développement d'un système à microprocesseurs.
English]
  Microprocessor system development/Alain Amghar; preliminary
pages translated by John C. C. Nelson.
    p. cm.
  Translation of: Méthodes de développement d'un système à
microprocesseurs.
  "March 1989."
  Includes bibliographical references and index.
  ISBN 0-13-582750-7 (pbk.)
  1. Microprocessors. 2. System design. I. Title.
QA76.5.A42713   1990
005.2'1--dc20

                          90-42884
                             CIP

British Library Cataloguing in Publication Data

Amghar, Alain
  Microprocessor system development.
  1. Microprocessor systems. Design
  I. Title II. Méthodes de développement d'un système à
microprocesseurs. *English*
  004.256

  ISBN 0-13-582750-7

---

1 2 3 4 5 94 93 92 91 90

Contents

Foreword

The appearance on the market of microprocessors, and other electronic circuits with a high degree of integration, has led to the development of many types of microcomputer and electronic control systems of all kinds.

There are many applications of microprocessor-based circuits such as machine control, process control, instrumentation, security monitoring and vehicle equipment. They affect equally the general public, the medical and military areas, industrial and airport installations, etc.

The hardware makes use of basic computer components and techniques which have been applied to computer design. Development requires rigorous analysis, sustained planning and methodical progression. Computer manufacturers have learned to master these aspects, but they are not necessarily familiar to the technical and commercial staff who have charge of a project. The constraints of price and completion date in 'microcomputing' increase the risk of leaving too great a part to improvization.

The aim of this book is to assist those who have the responsibility for developing and leading a project from design to final realization of a product, while maintaining quality and respecting delivery times. In this context, technical difficulties and personal conflicts will be encountered, and it will be necessary to resolve these.

M. Amghar details many selected topics in this book. These include hardware, since component manufacturers offer families of products which must be incorporated, and software for which the methodology is very time consuming. At each stage he shows how to co-ordinate the work, to inform and to facilitate the tasks of those who follow with accompanying documentation. Hence, from project specification to acceptance tests, the project is structured, the pitfalls are indicated and solutions are provided.

Some readers may find some methods place excessive demands on the available facilities, and that either there is not enough equipment or there is too short a timescale. They may be able to think of simpler solutions without ignoring the problems posed. It is most advisable to use this book in a supervisory role, asking the question 'Have I forgotten anything which will compromise the correct operation and the commercial success of my hardware?'

This work does not contain new coverage of microcomputers or languages –

numerous books take care of this. The experience of a project from start to finish does, however, need to be described. In an area where technology constantly brings new tools, the rules to be observed in accomplishing a coherent task which is communicable to others, such as colleagues, salespeople and users, vary little. Excellent advice will be found here together with a multitude of suggestions.

Annette Lauret
Engineer E.S.E.

Chapter 1

Project Specification

1.1 Introduction

The development of a microprocessor system is complex since it involves the co-operation of numerous partners. These include the originating company, which requires a product in response to its needs or commercial ambitions, the company which creates the product and may consist of teams from the originating company or an external supplier, the developers, who are electronic, mechanical and software engineers, and programmers, financiers and the administrative services of each organization.

The following chapters may be used to follow the step-by-step development of a product. A preliminary step will be described here which is very important because it conditions future development – the compilation of a 'project specification'.

The project specification is the main item which will permit invitations to tender to be submitted to possible suppliers. It describes the required product and the requirements which it must fulfil in terms of functions, cost, timescales and so on. It is fundamental, since the suppliers will make their offer on the basis of it. These companies must be able to justify their proposals using the same information, the same knowledge of the requirements and on the basis of sufficient information. It is, therefore, recommended that excessively rapid compilation of the project specification should be avoided. The customer must specify his requirements clearly and the supplier must not hesitate to indicate information which is missing from the technical, financial and contractual proposals. Subsequent communication difficulties and delays or surcharges due to last-minute modifications will thus be avoided.

1.2 Compilation of the Project Specification

The project specification is created from an internal requirement, a request from an external company or a need to produce a product for commercial purposes. When an organization takes the decision to produce a new product, it establishes a project specification or arranges for the customer to do so.

1

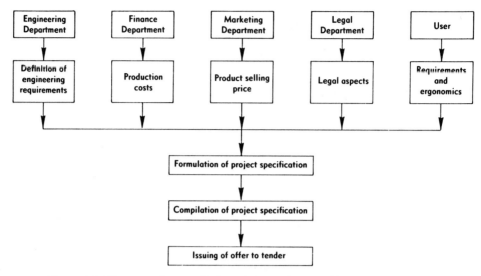

Figure 1.1 The stages in compilation of the project specification by the buyer.

Those involved in the production of the project specification are:

- The engineering department, which defines the various requirements and specifies the various functions.
- The end user, or a marketing agent, who defines the requirements and ergonomic aspects from the user's point of view.
- The commercial department, which determines the anticipated markets and maintains the product price within limits.
- The finance department, which considers the financial constraints in developing the new product with respect to budgetary provisions.
- The administrative or legal department, which defines the administrative and legal terms of the contract.

1.3   The Contents of a Project Specification

The project specification does not describe the manner in which the hardware will be realized. It defines the objectives, constraints and modes of operation. In general, a project specification contains the following:

1.3.1   The Destination and Objective of the Product

The main roles of the required product, particularly the specific requirements to which it responds (which may relate to industry, medicine, the general public and so on), must be clearly defined in this section.

1.3.2   The Required Functions

A definition of the functional requirements of the future product, including the following:

- A list of the various service functions expected of the product.
- The role of each function.
- Their hierarchy and interactions.
- Their relative values.
- A system block diagram.

This section is defined by the engineering department.

1.3.3   The Constraints Imposed on the Product

These are the constraints associated with physical details and operating conditions such as:

- Dimensions, weights, power consumption, performance, protection against power failures and breakdowns etc.
- The operating environment: noise, temperature, pressure, vibration etc.
- Required ergonomic features such as the type of display, the mechanical arrangement of the display, protection against reflections, persistence of vision, the type of keyboard, the slope of the keyboard, the arrangement and type of keys, the lengths of the various connecting cables etc.
- Special conditions which influence the construction techniques used, the hardware/software division for the execution of one or more functions of the product, the types of microprocessor, the programming languages used and equipment interconnection (the types of connectors, their location etc.).

All these items are evaluated by the engineering department which examines the feasibility of each one in the context of current techniques and technologies.

1.3.4   Monitoring the Progress of the Development Phases

The various stages which enable satisfactory progress of the project to be monitored are listed under this heading together with a list of the points to be checked at each of these stages. In the majority of cases, these stages consist of the following in the order given:
First phase:

- The supplier explains the technical solution adopted.
- The customer evaluates this solution from the point of view of feasibility and consistency of costs.

Second phase:

- The supplier demonstrates or provides a model and presents the operational features.
- The customer checks for correspondence between the solution and the specification and examines the characteristics of the components used.

Third phase:

- The first prototypes are produced and demonstrated.
- The customer confirms the tests performed on the prototypes and performs physical measurements such as levels, speeds, response times and so on.

Fourth phase:

- The product is finally accepted (see the section on acceptance testing).

The decisions taken at the end of each phase must be recorded, examples are:

- A decision whether to continue or stop; modification of functions by agreement of the partners.
- Changes to the completion date and cost.

This method serves to retain the constraints, monitor completion times and provide flexibility in the case of an unsuitable initial definition.

1.3.5 Acceptance Testing Methods

The object of acceptance testing is to check that the product conforms to the proposal. The project specification defines the form of the acceptance tests and includes such details as:

- The number of prototypes.
- The supporting documentation.
- The software in source and executable code format.
- A general definition of the quantitative and qualitative tests, particularly the product validation and evaluation tests (see Chapters 3 and 5); these tests enable the conformity of the product to the technical details in the project specification to be verified.

1.3.6 Development Sites

The site, or sites, where development will take place must be identified. If development is carried out on the supplier's premises, it is part of the job; otherwise, if it takes place on the customer's premises, it is contract work. Contract work is more costly than job work.

1.3.7   Completion Times

Either the total time to the final acceptance date or the separate times relating to a plan for monitoring the progress of the work according to the requirements described in Section 1.3.4 may be specified.

1.3.8   Guarantees

The duration and conditions of the equipment guarantee should be defined together with the parts covered by this guarantee.

1.3.9   Training and Transfer of 'Know How'

This section specifies the methods by which the customer organization acquires any required knowledge. This acquisition can take several forms:

- The engineers and technicians from the customer company form part of the development team on the premises of the company developing the product (this is rather rare).
- Intensive training on the product software and hardware are provided by the personnel who designed the product.
- The product is developed under contract at the customer's premises and in technical collaboration.

1.3.10   The Price Range and Methods of Payment

Prices and payment methods are detailed under this heading and include:

- Hardware costs.
- Software costs.
- The costs allowed for training.
- Maintenance costs for the guarantee period and beyond.

Note   Additional items can be included under this heading such as methods of revising an estimated cost and possible penalty clauses.

1.3.11   Terms of Non-concurrence

The items which define the property rights of the various sections of the developed prototype are listed under this heading together with the various non-concurrence clauses. In particular the geographical area involved (the country, countries or

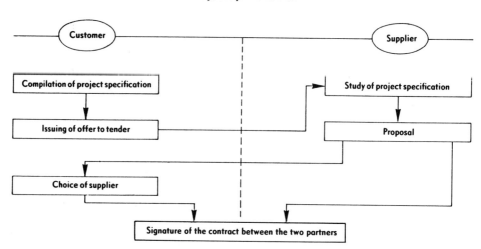

Figure 1.2 The route to selecting a supplier.

regions) and the terms of non-concurrence with delivery dates will be very precisely defined.

1.3.12 Legal Aspects

This heading lists disputes which could be taken to court, such as those associated with unsatisfactory interpretation and all other defects of form and content. Legal points likely to provide arbitration of the disputed matters should be indicated.

1.4 Signing the Contract

Once the project specification has been drawn up, it will be agreed by everyone who has participated in its compilation. The project specification can then be used for inviting tenders (see Fig. 1.2). Then, before making his choice of supplier and signing the contract between the two partners, the customer will examine the proposals made by the various suppliers who have responded to the invitation to tender.

1.5 Starting the Project

The company chosen to provide the product proceeds to establish the necessary administrative organization and technical arrangements (see Fig. 1.3) to realize the first prototypes in accordance with the route shown in Fig. 1.4 and detailed in the various chapters of this book.

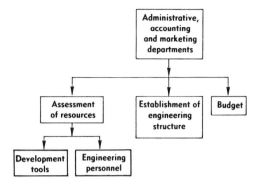

Figure 1.3 Setting up the structure necessary to realize a product.

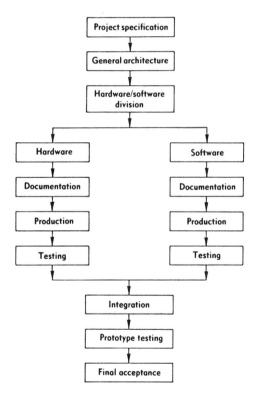

Figure 1.4 The various stages in the realization of the prototype.

Chapter 2 —————————————————————

Hardware/Software Division

General Architecture Documentation ——————————

2.1 Introduction

A start is made on defining the general architecture of the product from the project
specification (see Chapter 1). Decisions taken at this preliminary stage are essential
to the success of the product; they are also combined and described in a document
called the 'general architecture document'. The larger the project, in both hardware
and software, the more important this documentation becomes for the creation and
survival of the product; the time spent in writing this documentation will be regained
at every stage of development (particularly at the test and integration stage (see
Chapter 5)) and in subsequent updating.

The role of this documentation can be compared to the architect's file in building;
before starting construction of a house or any other building, it is necessary to have a
plan of the required construction. Each subsection of the building has its location, its
role and its interaction with other clearly defined subsections; the plan must permit
the overall consequences of subsequent addition or removal of one or more
subsections to be predicted.

The general architecture documentation is fundamental and will serve as a
reference throughout the development period and subsequently for every modification of the product.

2.2 Production of the General Architecture Documentation

The general architecture described in the documentation relates to interpretation of
the project specification in the light of essential computing criteria.

The following must be defined by the project specification:

- A general description of the product.
- The component functions required to achieve the system objectives.

8

- The nature of these functions and their general organization.
- The structure of the various functions.
- The interaction of these various functions.
- The execution times of the various functions.
- The file structure.
- The inputs and outputs and their type (digital, analogue, serial etc.) and signal characteristics (power, speed, time between voltage variations etc.)
- The routeing of input/output signals and the various functions which use these data.
- The routeing and processing of information streams.
- The use of data by the various functions.
- A list of tasks with priorities in the case of a multitask operating system.
- Communication between real-time tasks; possible constraints must be identified and documented.
- Interrupts and interrupt handling processes with priorities.
- Identification of conflicts (which could involve data, interrupt priorities – all possible cases of interrupt occurrence must be taken into account – tasks etc.).
- The user part of the interface (the set of utilities and commands associated with the latter must be listed).
- Fault tolerance specifications.
- Performance.
- Hardware/software division in functional terms.
- A list of electronic hardware components.
- Others such as the environment, power consumption limit, cost, etc.

In this documentation, the type of logic system chosen is also specified (the various types of logic system will be detailed in this chapter) together with the principal electronic hardware components (particularly the microprocessor type, if the logic system chosen is 'microprocessor programmable logic').

Checking of this documentation includes topics such as:

- Is it complete?
- What is the feasibility of the various functions and the system as a whole?
- Is it maintainable?
- Are there facilities for subsequent development?

These must be taken into account and rigorously analysed before proceeding to the development itself (see Chapters 3 and 4).

Choice of Logic System Type —————————————

2.3 Introduction

Realization of an electronics-based industrial system requires selection of a logic system which is best suited to the product. This selection is influenced by both technical and commercial factors. A logic system is a combination of logic elements realized with semiconductor components.

Certain factors, associated with the environment in which the product is required to operate, can decisively influence the choice of logic system to be used. These environmental factors can be:

- *Noise*: In this case components whose technology is susceptible to noise (for example ECL technology) should be avoided in favour of CMOS types or others which have a good noise immunity.
- *Radioactivity*: Preference should be given to the use of technologies which withstand a radioactive environment such as silicon-on-sapphire (SOS), since sapphire dissipates radiation, or perhaps silicon-on-insulator (SOI).
- *Power supply*: In an environment with frequent power cuts, the product must permit standby operation (alternatively it may be portable and powered by batteries). In this case a technology which consumes little energy and can support a relatively large power-supply variation, for example CMOS, should be used.

In addition to the purely technical aspect of the product, it is also necessary to choose a logic system, and consequently components, which lead to the lowest costs. Commercial aspects, including the quantity which it is hoped to sell, can enormously influence the choice of logic system in respect of the cost of components and ease of supply.

The success of a project can be ensured by discovering the least costly solution which meets the required specification.

2.4   Types of Logic System

The three types of logic system are:

- Wired logic.
- Microprocessor-based programmable logic.
- Minicomputer-based programmable logic.

2.4.1   Wired Logic

Wired logic involves interconnection of standard devices, each of which performs a limited number of functions, in order to realize one or more of the functions of an electronic product.

The 'wired logic' approach can be justified for a project by several factors such as:

- Speed.
- Complexity of the functions to be realized.
- Operating constraints (noise, power consumption etc.).
- Storage capacity.
- Cost.

Project requiring modest electronics

If the project in hand requires only about 30–50 standard logic devices, then, according to the constraints of operating speed, power consumption and product cost, the developer designs the product by first defining the type of technology most appropriate to the product (see Table 2.1) and then selecting the standard devices which best fulfil the required product functions. The development cost is, of course, very small in this case and the product can be available on the market quite quickly.

It should be noted that the characteristics of a particular technology develop very quickly and consequently the data for the various technologies given in Table 2.1 are for guidance only.

In certain cases, a combination of wired logic and programmed read only memory devices (EPROM/PROM) can be the most suitable solution, particularly if the microprocessor proves to have processing capacity disproportionate to the actual processing and logical requirements of the product.

Read only memory has the ability to provide output values on the data pins of the

Table 2.1 Comparison of the various standard electronic circuit technologies. (The characteristics given in this table relate to a logic gate, the speed relates to the signal propagation time.)

Technology	Speed nanosec.	Power consumption	Comments
CMOS	30	10 nW	The design of most microprocessors is based on CMOS. Derived from CMOS, Advanced CMOS Logic (ACL) achieves 3 ns for a consumption of less than 1 mW.
BiCMOS	0.4	7.5 mW	This recent technology is a combination of bipolar (TTL or ECL) and CMOS which provides high speed with low power consumption. An example is the Fairchild 256-Kbit SRAM with an access time of 10 ns and a consumption of less than 1 W.
H-MOS I	1	1 mW	Invented by Intel in 1977. High-performance
H-MOS II	0.4	1.2 mW	*n*-channel MOS (HMOS) is derived from CMOS.
H-MOS III	0.2	1.2 mW	
TTL	10	10 mW	Derived from TTL technology, Schottky Transistor Transistor Logic (STTL) achieves 3 ns for 20 mW. Low-power Schottky TTL (LSTTL) achieves 9 ns for 8 mW and Fairchild Advanced Schottky TTL (FAST) achieves 3 ns for 4 mW.
I²L	25	1 nW	Marketed since 1975, this provides a high integration density.
ECL	0.15	1 mW	Derived from ECL technology, ExCL achieves 0.2 ns for a power of 0.4 mW.
GaAs	<0.3	4 mW/gate for a speed of 230 ps	A new technology which is still under development. Examples are 100 MIPS microprocessors from RCA and Tektronix.

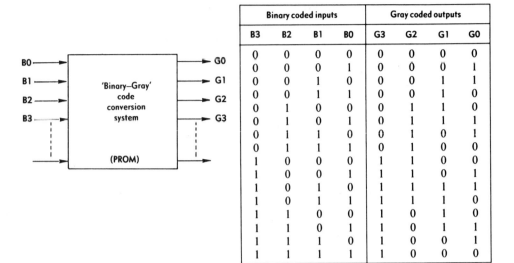

Binary coded inputs				Gray coded outputs			
B3	B2	B1	B0	G3	G2	G1	G0
0	0	0	0	0	0	0	0
0	0	0	1	0	0	0	1
0	0	1	0	0	0	1	1
0	0	1	1	0	0	1	0
0	1	0	0	0	1	1	0
0	1	0	1	0	1	1	1
0	1	1	0	0	1	0	1
0	1	1	1	0	1	0	0
1	0	0	0	1	1	0	0
1	0	0	1	1	1	0	1
1	0	1	0	1	1	1	1
1	0	1	1	1	1	1	0
1	1	0	0	1	0	1	0
1	1	0	1	1	0	1	1
1	1	1	0	1	0	0	1
1	1	1	1	1	0	0	0

Figure 2.1 (a) Binary code (B0–B3) to Gray code (G0–G3) conversion table. (b) A PROM used to convert from the binary input code B0–B3 to the Gray output code G0–G3.

memory device which correspond to input values on the address pins. Consequently, a programmed output value which is the solution of a logical equation, the result of a simple mathematical operation or a code conversion can be made to correspond to each binary input combination. Examples are binary-to-BCD code conversion, binary-to-Gray code conversion (see Fig. 2.1) and vice versa. However, the number of memory address pins of read only memories is limited to n inputs, where n is between 5 and 13 according to the memory device; this implies the possibility of decoding from 32 to 8192 combinations of 5–13 variables.

The most practical PROMS for this type of application are those with 5 or 6 inputs and 16 outputs. The type of read only memory used depends on the quantity of the product to be produced; EPROMS are used for debugging and very small quantity production, PROMS for a small run of products and ROMs for medium and large production runs.

Other programmable devices similar to PROMs and EPROMS can be selected, particularly for sequential logic; these devices are:

- EEPROMs (electrically erasable programmable read only memory). These are identical to EPROMs except that they can be erased electrically.
- PLAs (programmable logic array) and PALs (programmable array logic). PLAs have programmable AND and OR networks while with PALs only the OR network is programmable. The direct consequence is that PALs are faster (5–10 ns

difference for the same power consumption). The advantage of PLAs and PALs with respect to PROMs is that they provide a larger number of address bits.

- EPLDs (erasable programmable logic device). In contrast to PLAs and PALs, the contents of EPLDs can be erased with ultraviolet light and reprogrammed.
- EEPLDs (Electrically Erasable Programmable Logic Device). These are identical to EPLDs except that the contents can be erased electrically.

In the case where large-scale production is foreseen (more than 100 000 units), it is tempting to combine some or all of the standard parts used in the prototype into a single package. This approach requires development of the appropriate device by a manufacturer; the typical time to design this type of 'application specific integrated circuit' (ASIC) is around one or two years. This time has been considerably reduced, however, by the development and availability of powerful tools to assist in the design of 'custom chips'.

The stages in the design of this type of circuit are:

- Realization of a model to test the conformity of the logic and the circuit.
- Computer simulation of the circuit.
- Computer-assisted layout.
- Realization of masks for diffusion and connections.
- Realization of a prototype circuit.
- Testing functional operation and consistency of synchronization of timing signals.
- Pilot production.
- Series production.

The advantages of this type of device are as follows:

- Reduction of printed circuit area (miniaturization).
- Reduction of power consumption, particularly as a consequence of eliminating the unused sections of standard devices. This reduction leads to lower system power consumption or longer battery life in the case of a portable product.
- An increase in product performance as a result of reduced signal propagation time.
- Reduced cost of manufacturing the product.
- Facilitation of product test and maintenance.
- Protection against copying by competitors.

The disadvantages are:

- Relatively long delay in implementation and hence availability of the product on the market.
- Higher cost if the minimum economic quantity (around 100 000 units) is not achieved.
- Impossibility of modification during the lifetime of the device.

It should be noted that predefined networks in the form of 'gate arrays' may be used to reduce the number of SSI and MSI devices required.

Table 2.2 Comparison of various types of bit-slice microprocessor.

Microprocessor	Bus width bits	Technology	Speed in nanoseconds	Manufacturer	Comments
Am 2900	4	Bipolar	50–125	AMD	The most widely used bit-slice microprocessor.
MC 10800	4	ECL	50	Motorola	Applications are in graphics and superminicomputers.
MC 10900	8	ECL	50	Motorola	As for the MC 10800.
8X305	8	Bipolar	200 at 10 MHz	Signetics	
74AS888	8	Bipolar	46	Texas Instruments	Applications are in graphics and superminicomputers.
WORD-SLICE DSP	16	CMOS	100	Analog Device	For digital signal processing applications.
29300	32	Bipolar	90	AMD	Applications are in superminicomputers, graphics and communications. There is a CMOS version (AM 39300).
29400	32	ECL	40	AMD	As for the 29300.
WS 59032	32	CMOS	3–5 MIPs	Waferscale Integration	The power dissipated is 330 mW.
74AS8832	32	CMOS	50–75	Texas Instruments	As for the 74AS888.

Project requiring complex electronics and faster operation

If more than 50 logic devices are required, together with faster operation, these can execute a microinstruction in 50 ns (an example is the Motorola MC10800 in ECL technology). Several types of bit-slice microprocessor are available on the market (see Table 2.2).

A basic bit-slice microprocessor takes the form of an arithmetic and logic unit (ALU). To design a basic bit-slice microprocessor system, it is necessary to combine this device with the components necessary to form a central processing unit. These include a sequencer (which is generally available with the ALU), a micro-programming unit, various registers (equivalent to the internal registers of a standard microprocessor) and so on.

In addition to the speed of the technology used (ECL, TTL etc.) in comparison with that used in standard microprocessors (CMOS and NMOS), the design flexibility of a bit-slice microprocessor-based system allows the operating speed to be increased as follows:

- By using the pipeline technique which permits the execution time of instructions to be optimized.
- By reducing the execution time of certain functions by incorporating components in the central processing unit which permit them to be executed directly without additional instructions. An example of such a function is the multiplication operation which can be performed using a bipolar integrated technology B3018 in ECL technology. The 16-bit multiplication operation is executed in 5 ns (in contrast, the B3018 consumes 2.9 W).

In choosing a bit-slice microprocessor, in addition to the specific details of the product specification which determine the type of bit-slice microprocessor to be chosen, it is necessary to take account of the following:

- The availability of components to operate with the bit-slice microprocessor (such as a sequencer, a look-ahead carry circuit, a clock generator and so on).
- The availability of a development system and its accessories.
- Other facilities such as documentation, maintenance etc.

The disadvantages of bit-slice microprocessors are:

- The high development cost in comparison with standard microprocessors.
- Large space requirements.
- Complexity of realization due to:

  ⋆ The large number of operational circuits in comparison with a standard microprocessor.
  ⋆ Noise problems due to the high signal speed and particularly the technology used (typically ECL and TTL).
  ⋆ Interfacing between the various technologies in the case where the product requires this (ECL, TTL, CMOS etc.).
  ⋆ The possible use of microprogramming to create powerful instructions comparable with those found on the majority of standard microprocessors. (Microprograms are built up from microinstructions.)

- High power consumption in comparison with a standard microprocessor.

The advantages are:

- High speed of operation.
- The possibility of expanding the bus width, particularly the data bus, by putting microprocessors in parallel (see Fig. 2.2). When it is required to put several (more than two) bit-slice microprocesssors in parallel, this expansion can raise several problems which are primarily associated with the propagation speed of signals such as the carry. It is then necessary to use a carry look-ahead circuit.
- The possibility of using the pipeline technique which permits the instruction to be executed much more rapidly than on the majority of standard microprocessors (particularly 8-bit microprocessors). The majority of 32-bit microprocessors (for example the 80386) already use this technique which significantly increases their performance.

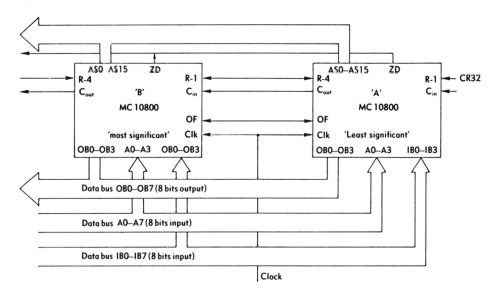

Figure 2.2 Connection of two bit-slice microprocessors (MC10800 of 4 bits) in parallel to produce an 8-bit system. Microprocessor A forms the four least significant bits (XX3–XX0) and microprocessor B the most significant ones (XX7–XX4); the signals involved in this configuration are IB0–IB3 and A0–A3, the input bus, and OB0–OB3, the output bus.

The carry output signal C_{out} of processor A and carry input C_{in} of processor B are connected together to permit transfer of the carry from the less significant part of the data to the more significant part.

Signals R-1 of processor A and R-4 of processor B are sent to a shift register and are used for the right- and left-shift operations.

The overflow signals OF are also fed to a status register (overflow indicator).

Zero Detect ZD is connected to the status register; this signal indicates when the data are equal to zero.

The 16 signals AS0–AS15 are fed to the microprogram unit and the control unit; these signals control the various operations of the ALU (MC10800) (addition, subtraction, shifting etc.) and are activated by the microprogram unit (by means of micro-instructions) and the control unit.

- The possibility of defining specific functions in wired logic instead of microprogramming them as is the case with some standard microprocessors; however, several 32-bit microprocessors already have functions such as multiplication in wired logic.
- The possibility of defining an instruction set specific to the product manufacturer and thus permitting creation of products which are compatible with other products already on the market while retaining very high operating speeds with respect to available products.

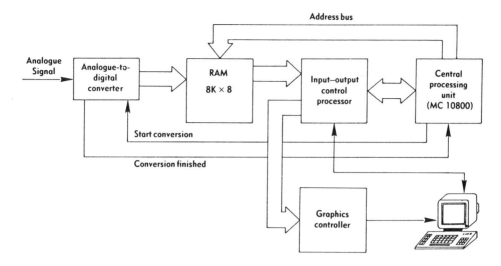

Figure 2.3 Block diagram of a hardware system designed around the MC 10800 bit-slice microprocessor for processing a video signal.

An example of the use of a bit-slice microprocessor is shown in Fig. 2.3; the objective is to perform algorithm-based processing such as the Fast Fourier and Hilbert transforms and digital filtering of a video signal.

Before being stored the signal is converted into digital form by means of an 8-bit analogue-to-digital converter; the conversion speed of the latter must be at least twice the video signal frequency. Various types of converter having a conversion time able to support video signal frequencies are available on the market. Examples are the SONY CXA 1066K 8-bit analogue-to-digital converter which has a conversion rate of 100 MHz and the Analog Devices AD9703 8-bit digital-to-analogue converter which has a conversion rate of 300 MHz and a power dissipation of 1.1 W.

The data storage memory must be fast (such as fast SRAM – see the section on static RAMS in Chapter 4, or RAMs in ECL technology).

The processing unit uses a Motorola 4-bit bit-slice microprocessor, the MC10800 in ECL technology, as the basic element. Interconnection of the two ALUs to form an 8-bit data bus is detailed in Fig. 2.2. The block diagram of the contents of the processing unit is given in Fig. 2.4. The signal thus processed in the central processing unit can be displayed on a screen.

In the majority of cases, the design of a bit-slice microprocessor-based system involves building a central processing unit which corresponds to the architecture of a standard mircoprocessor (see Fig. 2.4); this consists of the arithmetic and logic unit, the microprogramming unit, the control unit, the sequencer, the status register and various other registers (instruction register, accumulators, stack pointer, program counter etc.).

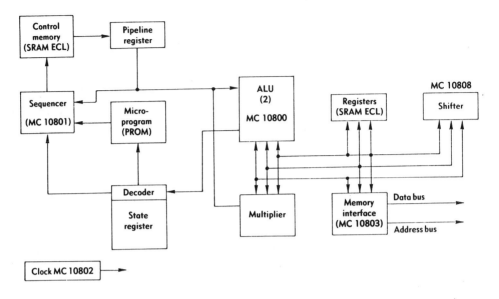

Figure 2.4 Central processing unit based on the MC 10800 bit-slice microprocessor. The MC10803 device permits generation of address and data buses such as those associated with standard microprocessors. The MC10808 shifter permits the execution of various data shifting and rotating operations. A (wired) multiplier is added to increase the speed of execution of multiplication instructions.

Processors for signal processing

Digital signal processing (DSP) devices are generally similar in their internal architecture to standard microprocessors; in contrast the instruction set is much more oriented towards dedicated signal-processing applications (for example, a 16×16-bit multiplication takes 240 ns and a 32-point Fast Fourier transform (FFT) requiring around 210 instructions takes 700 μs with the NEC μPD7720).

In the case where the product to be realized is intended for signal-processing applications (for example: speech synthesis and recognition, sonar, seismic, ultrasonic, radar and X-ray signal analysis etc.) the use of a DSP device can be the most judicious solution.

In order to increase the operating speed of the product, the possibility of interconnecting a standard microprocessor and a DSP device can be worth while to free the microprocessor from processing specific to the signal (see Fig. 2.5).

2.4.2 Microprocessor-based Programmable Logic

Once a microprocessor has been chosen as the logic system best suited to development of the product, it remains to select the most appropriate micro-

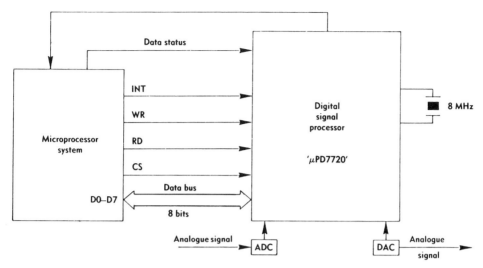

Figure 2.5 Interfacing a DSP device (μPD7720) to a microprocessor-based system. Serial analogue-to-digital converters (to accept the signal to be processed) and serial digital-to-analogue converters (to output the processed signal) are included in this diagram to form a complete dedicated signal processing system. In this way, the μPD7720, under the control of a microprocessor, is responsible for acquisition, processing and analogue output of the processed signal.

processor from the multitude of devices available on the market. The choice is determined by the features of the product to be realized and its technical specification. The selection criteria are generally based on the following factors.

Data bus width

The data bus width determines the precision of calculations and data manipulation; the greater the bus width, the greater the precision for a given number of transfers. The most widely used data bus widths are presently 4, 8, 16 and 32 bits (see Tables 2.3–2.6). Some microprocessors offer the facility in their internal structure (particularly in the internal registers) of bus widths twice that available on the device pins; this is a great advantage for processing and manipulating data since it permits an increase in precision while limiting the number of instructions (an example is the MC68000 16-bit microprocessor with an internal 32-bit structure).

Internal structure

The internal structure of a microprocessor can offer certain advantages with respect to other microprocessors, such as:

• The number of registers: some applications require the use of several registers, the unavailability of registers will increase the number of memory accesses, slow down execution and encourage the use of a 'scratch-pad' memory.

- Use of the pipeline technique (generally available in 32-bit microprocessors).
- The availability in the microprocessor package of certain functions such as a memory management unit (MMU) which permits address translation to be speeded up due to a reduction in signal propagation delays (see the section on memory management units in Chapter 4).

Memory capacity

Some application programs require a large memory capacity; the microprocessor selected must provide a memory capacity which permits such programs to execute normally by providing virtual memory management facilities or an MMU.

The actual read/write memory requirements may be uncertain or incorrectly estimated at this stage; however, an error of judgement in this matter can have consequences which are difficult to rectify.

The instruction set

Although the instruction sets of different microprocessors of comparable power (4, 8, 16 and 32 bits) are generally similar, some microprocessors have additional

Table 2.3 Comparison of various types of 4-bit microprocessor.

Micro-processor	Technology	Speed in microseconds	Power consumption	Manufacturer	Comments
75XX	CMOS	2.44–7.6	300 μA at 5 V 150 μA at 3 V	NEC	Widely used in calculators and miniaturized products.
75X	CMOS	0.95–15.3	300 μA at 5 V 150 μA at 3 V	NEC	A development system is the Evakit 7520/7500
COP400	NMOS and CMOS	14–64	3 mA to 120 μA (at 2.4 V)	National Semi-conductor	A microcomputer which contains a microprocessor, memory and input/output interfaces. A development system is the MOLE.
TMS 1000	PMOS and CMOS	15–60	90 mW at 15 V	Texas Instruments	A microcomputer which contains a microprocessor, RAM, ROM and input/output interfaces.

Table 2.4 Comparison of various types of 8-bit microprocessor.

Micro-processor	Technology	Speed in microseconds	Power consumption	Manufacturer	Comments
COP800	CMOS	1	15 mA	National Semi-conductor	A microcomputer which contains a microprocessor, memory and input/output interfaces. A development system is the MOLE.
8051/8052 8751	NMOS and CMOS	1	200 mW	Intel	A microcomputer which contains a microprocessor, memory and input/output interfaces. Development systems are: ICE-5100/252 on an Intellec or IBM-PC, ICE-51 on an Intellec, EMV-51A on an iPDS etc.
8080/8085	NMOS and CMOS	2	1 W	Intel	The clock circuit is incorporated in the 8085. Development systems are: Intellec, iPDS, Tektronix 8002A, Futuredata, H.P. HP64000 etc.
Z80	NMOS and CMOS	1 to 8.8	60 mA to 90 mA 15 mA (CMOS)	Zilog	A development system is the SGS UX-8/22.
6800/6802/ 6809/6309	NMOS and CMOS	1 to 5	−500 mW	Motorola	The clock circuit and memory are included in the 6802. The 6809 has an internal 16-bit structure. A development system is the Exorciser.
6500/1 65C124 50740 37700	NMOS and CMOS	2	300 μA to 100 mA	Rockwell W.D.C. Mitsubishi	Several versions are available with ROM, RAM, I/O interfaces, an A/D converter and LCD drivers. Development systems are: The Rockwell LCE System, The Mitsubishi PC 4000E, The Apple II (Toolbox design) Western Design Center.

Table 2.5   Comparison of various types of 16-bit microprocessor.

Micro-processor	Technology	Speed	Power consumption	Manufacturer	Comments
HPC 16040	CMOS	240 nanosec	20 mA	National Semi-conductor	Several versions are available with I/O interfaces, RAM, EEPROM, specific gate arrays and HDLC, CRT, DMA, SCSI and Ethernet controllers. Development systems are MOLE on an IBM-PC/XT/AT, Apple II, Intellec or VAX (UNIX/VMS).
8086/80186	NMOS and CMOS	0.37 μs at 8 MHz	10 mA/MHz	Intel	Development systems are: Intellec Tektronix 8002A etc.
80286	NMOS	200 ns at 10 MHz	600 mA at 5 V	Intel	As for the 80186.
68000	NMOS and CMOS	Clock cycle: 125 nanosec	1.2 W typical	Motorola	Development systems are: Exormacs, MICE 2+ on an IBM-PC
Z8000	NMOS	0.3 to 1 at 10 MHz	3 to 4 W	Zilog	A development system is the Z-Scan 8000.
32016	NMOS and CMOS	0.3 to 7.6	1.5 W	National Semi-conductor	Development systems are: VR32, SYS32/20 on an IBM-PC, ISE32 on a VAX.
V30	CMOS	6 to 8 μs for one multiplication or division.	500 mW at 5 MHz	NEC	A development system is the NEC MD-086
IMS T212	CMOS	10 MIPS	0.7 W	Inmos	A development system is IMS D701 on an IBM-PC.
8089	NMOS	DMA transfer at 1.25 MB/sec	350 mW at 5 V	Intel	A processor specifically for input/output control. A development system is the Intellec.

Table 2.6 Comparison of various types of 32-bit microprocessor.

Micro-processor	Technology	Speed	Power consumption	Manufacturer	Comments
80386	CMOS	3 to 4 MIPs for 16 MHz	400 mA at 16 MHz	Intel	Contains microprocessor and MMU. Development systems are: ICE386 on an Intellec, MICE386 on an IBM-PC etc.
68020	NMOS and CMOS	5 MIPS at 24 MHz	1.5 W	Motorola	Development systems are: HDS-400 Exormacs.
32032	NMOS and CMOS	0.3 to 7.6 μs	1.5 W	National Semi-conductor	Development systems are: VR32, ISE32 on an IBM-PC
WE32100	CMOS	3 to 4 MIPS	0.8 W	ATT	Development system is WE32 1DS.
Z80000	NMOS	12.5 MIPS at 25 MHz	3 to 4 W	Zilog	Contains microprocessor and MMU.
IMS T414	CMOS	50 ns at 20 MHz	0.9 W	Inmos	The transputer, inspired by RISC architecture. Development systems are: IMS D701-4 on an IBM-PC. IMS D600 on a VAX/VMS.
34010	CMOS	160 ns		Texas Instruments	Used mainly as a graphics controller. Development systems are: TMS 34010 XDS/22 on an IBM-PC.
2900 RISC	CMOS	17 MIPS	1.5 W	AMD	A RISC architecture micro-processor.
CLIPPER	CMOS	5 MIPS to 33 MIPS		Fairchild	The internal architecture is similar to RISC.
NCR32	NMOS	150 ns		NCR Corp.	A microprocessor which can be microprogrammed by means of an external memory device. Used in the NCR 9300 computer. Development system is the Hivel Technology DS370.

instructions which can be very useful during software development. The availability of such instructions enable program length to be reduced and consequently facilitates software testing and software/hardware integration.

In some cases the comparison should also include the various available addressing modes of the microprocessors.

Speed

In addition to the mean duration of the various instructions and the memory access times, it is important to compare the execution speed of a given function (such as multiplication, division, data block transfer etc.) on the various possible microprocessors. However, speed is only really significant through the execution of 'benchmark' programs which permit the execution times and processing capabilities of each microprocessor to be checked. These programs are generally available from the microprocessor manufacturer or distributor.

The clock frequency of a microprocessor should be used only as a guide; it is not significant unless the speed-dependent elements mentioned above have been taken into account and analysed.

Price and availability

The investigation of price and availability must not be restricted to the microprocessor itself but should also take account of the following:

- The full set of devices to be used including peripheral interface devices (synchronous serial, asynchronous, disk etc.), the arithmetic coprocessor, memory management units, controllers (for graphics, DMA, dynamic memory, networks etc.), the clock generator etc.
- The set of development tools which will be necessary, particularly the development system and its accessories (hardware and software).

Comments
- If the components and/or tools are not available at the start of the design, about six months additional to the manufacturer's quoted release date should be allowed. Peripheral interface devices and other controllers are generally very late in comparison with the availability of the microprocessor itself.
- For military applications, the same steps may be taken while verifying that the range of components operates to the military specification.

Unusual facilities

These are the characteristics which will be analysed in terms of the requirements of the product to be realized:

Possible use of multiprocessors. The majority of 32-bit microprocessors support multiprocessor applications. It is important to determine the capabilities and limitations of multiprocessors while selecting the microprocessor. This capability can be evidenced by the availability of pins on the microprocessor which permit interaction with other microprocessors.

Interrupt management facility. The number of interrupts and the availability of non-maskable interrupts.

Multitasking facilities. A multitasking system provides the user with a facility to execute several tasks at the same time (for example, editing a file and initiating a 'submit' file which contains a sequence of commands). The operating system simulates several processors by offering a 'virtual processor' for each task. At each instant, the operating system assigns the real processor to a virtual processor which consequently executes the task associated with the latter processor. To maintain the illusion of one processor per task, the operating system switches the real processor frequently between the various virtual processors. The number of simultaneous tasks is, however, still limited.

Through its architecture, a microprocessor can facilitate the writing of operating systems with an instruction structure which permits construction of identification fields for each task (a 'Task Control Block') together with the generation of a task management system.

Availability of a protected mode. The protected mode permits microprocessors provided with this facility to execute several programs while avoiding conflicts

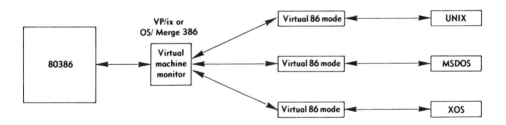

Figure 2.6 Using the characteristics of the virtual 86 mode, which is a subset of the protected mode of the 80386, the latter can execute three operating systems at the same time (for example: UNIX, MSDOS and XOS (XOS can be an operating system specific to the product designer)). The operation of these three operating systems is initialized as three distinct and protected tasks. The programs contained in an operating system can operate in multitask mode, execute input/output instructions and instructions associated with interrupts, thereby causing conflicts. To resolve these conflicts, a software module, called a virtual machine monitor, can be used (this type of module is available from Interactive Systems Corporation and Phoenix Technology under the name VP/ix, or from Locus Computing Corporation under the name OS/Merge 386. The role of this module is to provide arbitration in the case of the conflicts mentioned above while simulating these instructions.

When an instruction mentioned above creates a conflict, this software module inspects bit b17 (VM86 flag) of the status register of the 80386: if the system is in the process of executing a task, the virtual machine monitor takes control, simulates the instruction used and returns control to the virtual 86 mode.

between them (examples are ill-timed modification of the status register and access to reserved areas of a program). The availability of a protection system is particularly necessary for microprocessors having more than one gigabyte of physical address space, for multitask operating systems and products which can operate with several operating systems.

The facility for simultaneous execution of several different operating systems. (An example is the 80386 – see Fig. 2.6.)

Special-purpose microprocessors and microcomputers

The vast majority of microprocessors are based on CMOS technology. With the development of this technology, more and more functions are being included in the microprocessor package. Examples are: direct memory access (DMA), input/output interfaces, analogue-to-digital and digital-to-analogue converters, liquid crystal display (LCD) drivers etc. (see Fig. 2.7).

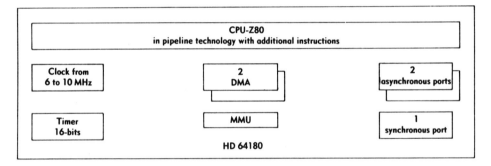

Figure 2.7 The Hitachi HD64180 microprocessor contains the equivalent of a Z80 designed using the pipeline technique, the instruction set of the Z80 enriched with additional instructions, a clock circuit, two DMA circuits, a programmable 16-bit timer, a memory management unit (MMU), two serial asynchronous ports and one serial synchronous port.

Some microprocessors are specific to one function; for example, the Intel 8089 special-purpose microprocessor for input/output processing and management – an 'input/output processor' (IOP).

The loss of ports when using these devices is compensated by a reduction in congestion on the printed circuit and a reduction in power consumption. This tendency has now progressed to the extent that microprocessors, such as the IBM 32-bit microprocessor, are being designed to execute a system program which accepts 102 mainframe instructions. The term 'system on a chip' illustrates this new concept.

Power consumption

The power dissipated can be fundamental, particularly for portable products which require a battery supply and consequently a maximum of autonomous operation. Microprocessors in CMOS technology with low power consumption and able to operate in stand-by mode are clearly the most suitable. With the high density of integration which it offers, CMOS technology facilitates the design of specific very large-scale integrated circuit (VLSI) components which permit the product to be miniaturized.

Company expertise

The expertise of a company with one or more microprocessors can also influence the choice, particularly if several microprocessors can conveniently meet the required product specification. Another aspect is the relationship which may exist between the organization which designs the product and the microprocessor manufacturer.

Second source supply of the chosen device family

The availability of second sources has the advantage of guaranteeing the availability of devices and raises the possibility of price negotiation. The continued sale of the microprocessor or microprocessors will also be assured.

2.4.3   Minicomputer-based Programmable Logic

With the appearance of new microprocessors, particularly those of 32 bits, the boundary between microcomputers and minicomputers is difficult to define.

The choice of a minicomputer is influenced principally by commercial objectives and technical requirements which standard microprocessors cannot satisfy. The principal ones are:

- A requirement for large memory capacity which standard microprocessors cannot provide.
- A search for very high operating speeds in comparison with those of standard microprocessors.
- The need for a very powerful instruction set.
- The need for a multi-user system with a large number of simultaneous users. For example, more than 128 users who are able to access a master station simultaneously from secondary stations.

The design of minicomputers is based on one of the following approaches.

The use of bit-slice microprocessors

Until the recent introduction of two other techniques (RISC architecture and parallel architecture) the great majority of minicomputer central processing units were based on bit-slice microprocessors which, in spite of their operational complexities, provide a high performance and free choice of data width. Far from being outdated, this technology is still used and contributes to the development of new bit-slice microprocessors, which are even faster and have wider data buses. Current developments in GaAs bit-slice microprocessors are also making foreseeable the design of faster and more powerful minicomputers using bit-slice microprocessors operating at very high speed. One example is the RCA 8-bit bit-slice microprocessor in GaAs technology which can achieve a speed of 100 MIPs with a 200 MHz clock.

By way of example, a 32-bit minicomputer achieving up to 50 MIPs can be designed around an 8-bit ECL bit-slice microprocessor by using the following in the central processing unit:

- Four TIE 10X888GB devices for the arithmetic and logic unit (an instruction cycle takes 20 ns).
- RAMs in ECL technology (access time 6 ns for the various registers and memory monitoring).
- TIE-10173s for the pipeline register.
- TIE 10X890s for the sequencer.
- Programmable logic devices (PLD), which can have response times of the order of 3–5 ns, for the various decoding operations.

The use of RISC architecture microprocessors

Microprocessors with reduced instruction set computer (RISC) architecture are distinguished from conventional microprocessors by the following points:

- The instruction set is optimized and includes a limited number of simple instructions and, in particular, a limited number of addressing modes. In spite of this reduction, a RISC architecture microprocessor is always a good choice for most types of processing since it is faster than conventional microprocessors.
- Decomposition of each instruction into micro-instructions is hardware controlled; there is no microprogramming unit and this causes a significant increase in the speed of execution of instructions.
- The basic instruction is executed in a single clock cycle.
- The number of registers is large; with the exception of LOAD and STORE instructions which require memory reference, all other instructions perform their processing by reference to registers. In particular, problems of passing parameters between procedures are resolved by using registers.
- The pipeline technique permits the instruction execution time to be optimized. Notice, however, that this arrangement also exists in some standard 32-bit microprocessors such as the 80386.

Manufacturers of microprocessors based on RISC architecture are IBM, Hewlett-Packard, Fairchild, Mips Computer, Digital Equipment, Cypress Semiconductors, AT&T etc.

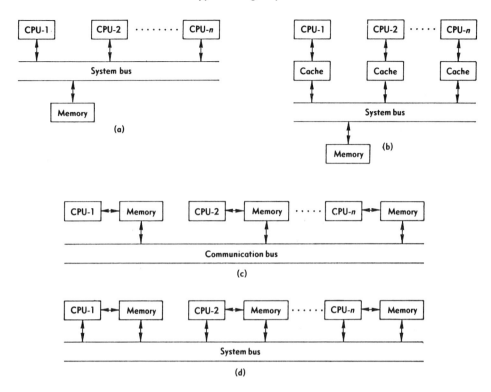

Figure 2.8 Block diagrams of various types of multiprocessor system interconnection. (a) Sharing of a single global memory: all the microprocessors share a common memory, intermicroprocessor communication is via a system bus. (b) Sharing of a global memory via a 'cache': this is the same as (a) except that access to the common memory is made through a cache memory, which enables the frequency of access to the global memory to be reduced. (c) Interprocessor communication network: each microprocessor has its own memory, interprocessor exchanges occur as messages on a communication bus. This type of configuration is used particularly in systems with parallel MIMD architecture. (d) Shared local memory: each microprocessor has its own memory but can also access other microprocessor memories via a system bus.

This type of microprocessor is also suitable for military applications; of particular interest are RISC architecture microprocessors in gallium arsenide (GaAs) technology.

The use of multiprocessors (see Fig. 2.8)

These are systems which use a set of microprocessors from the same or different families; the majority are of 32 bits such as the MC68020, NS32032 and 80386.
Two types of architecture can be distinguished:

- Several microprocessors which execute several distinct tasks at the same time.

- Several processes, which relate to a given task, can be performed simultaneously be several microprocessors; with this architecture, called parallel, there are four types of approach:

  ⋆ SISD (single instruction–single data) – each processor executes a single instruction on one set of data.

  ⋆ SIMD (single instruction–multiple data) – several microprocessors execute the same operation on several sets of data. This approach enables the speed of execution to be increased, particularly for performing scientific calculations. This technique is found in large computers such as the IBM 360/11, Cray I, Control Data 6600 etc.

  ⋆ MISD (multiple instruction–single data) – several microprocessors execute different operations on the same data.

  ⋆ MIMD (multiple instruction–multiple data) – several microprocessors operate independently of each other and on different data. These microprocessors can, for example, operate simultaneously with different operating systems. Examples are FX/8, Multimax, Concurrent 3200 MPS, Sequent Balance 8000, Flex/32 etc.

A computer or minicomputer with parallel architecture can combine different microprocessors; the most widely used are standard 32-bit and 32-bit RISC

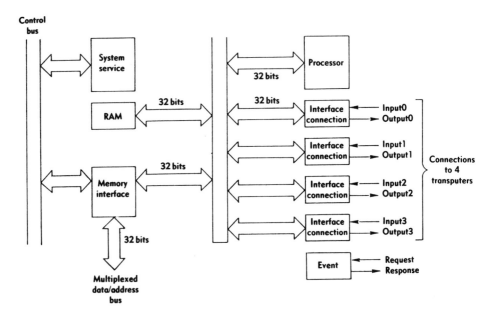

Figure 2.9 Internal structure of the T414 transputer. The 'memory interface' block permits direct addressing of more than 4 gigabytes.

architecture microprocessors and those inspired by RISC architecture such as the Inmos T414 and T800 transputers.

Some manufacturers use their own special microprocessors or a combination of special and standard microprocessors with bit-slice microprocessors. The number of microprocessors has no theoretical limit.

Note A transputer is a microcomputer which has its own local memory and communication lines which permit links to be made with four other transputers (see Fig. 2.9).

Software/hardware Division ————————————

2.5 Mono- and Multiprocessor Systems

The number of microprocessors to be used in a product is determined by:

- The ratio which defines the rate of occupation of a microprocessor. If this rate proves to be high, it is appropriate to consider a multiprocessor system.
- The information flow.

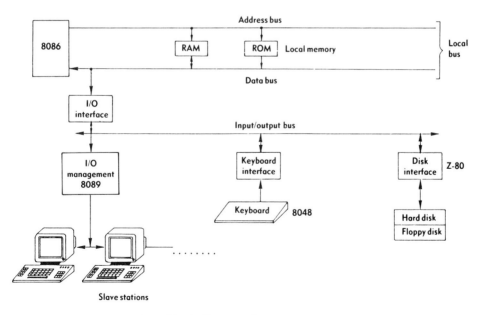

Figure 2.10 Block diagram of a multiprocessor system.

- The response times.
- Performance requirements which encourage distribution of different functions among various microprocessors. The majority of multi-user products require a multiprocessor system, independently of the fact that each station can have its own microprocessor or processors.

An example of a multi-user product is shown in Fig. 2.10; it consists of a master microprocessor dedicated to processing application software (accounting, word processing etc.), a keyboard management microprocessor, a microprocessor to interface with the hard and soft disk drive units and a microprocessor to control input/output and interstation communication (the 8089 is an example of a special-purpose microprocessor for input/output control).

2.6 Software/hardware Division

Once the type of logic system is defined, and if the choice is based on a microprocessor or microcomputer system, the functions to be performed are divided between those which must be executed by the hardware and those which must be executed by the software. In this division, four important factors must be taken into account:

- Feasibility of the function and its cost – the hardware solution sometimes has technical advantages. Examples are:
  - ⋆ Timers: To avoid monopolizing the microprocessor (for example using loops to cause a periodic action), a programmable timer circuit can be used.
  - ⋆ Mathematical calculations: Execution by software takes a long time in comparison with a mathematical coprocessor. The availability of such a device in the product will relieve the central microprocessor and significantly improve the performance (speed) of the product in addition to facilitating software debugging.

  The relative costs should then be evaluated. The cost is related to the complexity of the function to be realized – the more complex the function, the higher the cost of software development. In contrast, a software solution reduces the equipment costs; consequently, if the product is to be produced in large numbers, it is important to perform as many functions as possible in software.
- Subsequent development: When development of the product can be foreseen, modifications (at the design, production and installation stages) are easier and of lower cost in software than in hardware.
- Speed: A given function executed by electronic components is faster than when executed by software.
- Space: The software solution requires less space than that realized by an electronic device.

2.7 Memory Size and RAM/ROM Division

The software managers provide an estimate of the required RAM and ROM capacities. These initial values are, of course, approximate and reflect the expected volume of code and data; these values will later be determined more precisely. The hardware managers generally make provision for greater capacities on the memory boards and also leave space for possible extensions.

2.8 Memory Map Definition

The memory map specifies the distribution of the addresses available on the address bus among the various system components – the different types of memory (RAM and ROM), buffers for links to peripherals and special devices such as data converters. The address areas thus defined by the hardware designers (see Fig. 2.11) will be used for software development.

To accelerate the design stages, the hardware designers also compile a file which contains a list of the addresses of programmable electronic devices such as controllers, peripheral interfaces, data converters, multiplexers and so on. A meaningful name (a label) is assigned to each address (see Fig. 2.12). This permits the software designer to produce programs using these labels and ultimately to update the file containing the labels by modifying the appropriate addresses; the latter file is then sent to the hardware section.

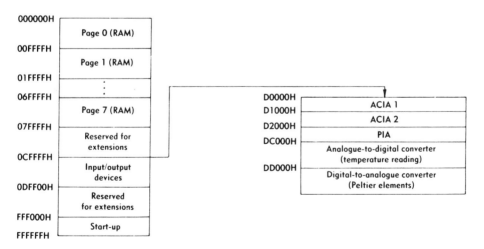

Figure 2.11 Memory map. *Note*: ACIA and PIA respectively denote 'asynchronous communications interface adaptor' and 'peripheral interface adaptor'.

ACIA1S	EQU	$D0008	CONTROL OR STATUS REGISTER OF ACIA1
ACIA1D	EQU	$D0009	DATA REGISTER OF ACIA1
ACIA2S	EQU	$D1008	CONTROL OR STATUS REGISTER OF ACIA2
ACIA2D	EQU	$D1009	DATA REGISTER OF ACIA2
PIADA	EQU	$D2000	DDRA/ORA
PIACA	EQU	$D2002	CRA
PIADB	EQU	$D2001	DDRB/ORB
PIACB	EQU	$D2003	CRB

Figure 2.12 File containing address assignments.

2.9 Mechanical Design and Construction

This part will not be treated in this book; however, its importance should be noted in every computer project.

Basic factors such as the dimensions and form of the product, the board dimensions and location and the power supply must be defined at the start. This permits the hardware section to define the components to be mounted on each board and the power requirements for autonomy of supply in the case of a portable product. As a consequence, the mechanical feasibility of the product can be checked for those cases where dimension limits are imposed.

2.10 Subsequent Stages

2.10.1 Software (see Chapter 3)

The software section starts by formalizing the specification documentation and analysing each product function before initiating subdivision into modules (see Chapter 3); this is followed by coding and testing (see Chapters 3 and 5).

2.10.2 Hardware (see Chapter 4)

The hardware section initiates:

- A list of the inputs and outputs with the characteristics of each signal, the number of LSI peripheral interface components to be used (if this type of device has been chosen) and a definition of any additional circuits required to adapt these signals to ensure compatibility with the voltage levels, power, speed etc. of an industrial system.

- A search for components which meet the requirements of the various functions to be realized including the following:

  * Microprocessor(s).
  * LSI and VLSI components associated with the microprocessor and other peripheral circuits (decoders, bus buffers etc.).
  * Memory components (DRAM or SRAM, PROM or EPROM etc.).
  * Special function components (arithmetic coprocessor(s), multipliers/dividers, analogue-to-digital converters, digital-to-analogue converters etc.).
  * Peripheral interface components (parallel, serial, floppy and hard disk drivers, graphics, etc.).

- A choice of the type of bus to be used on the mother board (this bus can be special or standard).
- A choice of the various types of connectors to be used on the boards.
- The production of block diagrams of the various boards constituting the product.
- Specification of the memory map.

Chapter 3 ———————————————————————————

Software Design

The object of this chapter is to cover the aspects of software organization and architecture and the steps to be followed before programming or writing the code for a program. The aim is not to teach programming, it is assumed that programming techniques are known to the reader.

During the ordered development of a microprocessor-based product, the software follows the production of the general architecture documentation and the software/hardware division (see Fig. 3.1); these are defined in Chapter 2.

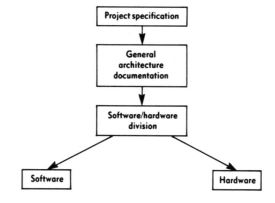

Figure 3.1 Location of the software design stage in the product realization process.

Introduction ———————————————————————————

Software development plays an important part in the overall cost of realizing a microprocessor-based product; this part, far from decreasing, increases with the development of microprocessors and the complexity of the projects to be realized.

To reduce this cost, various types of software production methodology have been proposed and applied by the companies which specialize in software design.

All these methods have the objective of:

- Reducing the cost of software development, particularly at the debugging and software/hardware integration stages (which form 70% of the cost of software development.)
- Reducing, as far as possible, the number of errors on delivery of the product. (The greater the progress from the first phase of software creation, the greater the cost of correcting an error).
- Reusing software developed for other projects; this permits the costs of software design and development to be made profitable and hence productivity to be increased.

Ideally in software development it would be possible to observe the following five objectives:

Design. Mastery of the software by the designer and also by a third party; this is facilitated if every program is accompanied by documentation and a clear and uniform listing with detailed comments. Any programmer must easily be able to deduce the function of a piece of software from its organization and comments. (Examples of documentation and presentation of software listings are given later in this chapter.)

Modification/Extension. It must be possible to make any modification due to development of the product quickly without involving other programs; this requires a structured organization (see the section on structured programming in this chapter).

Portability. Reuse of programs from other products provides a gain in software productivity. Portability is associated with program structure; those parts of the software which can be reused must be identified in the first phases of development.

Maintenance. The software must be easily comprehensible and easy to test. The ease or difficulty of maintenance is directly related to the type of production methodology used together with the rigour with which this methodology has been applied during the development process (important features are software modularity, ease of testing and so on).

Use. The software must be user friendly. Whatever the quality and performance of software, if its operation is too complicated it will tend to be rejected by the end-user (see pages 43 and 70).

The methodology proposed in this chapter enables the work load which is necessary for software design to be evaluated: this methodology includes several successive steps (see Fig. 3.2) not only for software development but also, above all, for correct use throughout the development process (coding, testing and maintenance) and in subsequent development of the product. Each step is started only when the preceding step has been properly validated (see page 69).

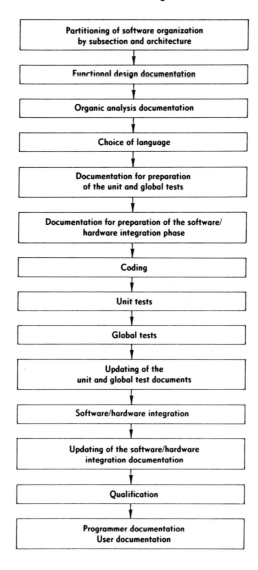

Figure 3.2 Software design stages.

In the production of software, the following factors must be taken into account and observed by the software development team from the start of the project:

- Uniformity in the presentation of programs and the interfaces between modules and subroutines.
- Clear identification of the elements to be realized.

- Software modifications, when they are necessary, must be accompanied by an updating of the documents associated with the modified programs. If the modifications relate to external specifications, all aspects of the project must be reviewed.
- Uniformity of terminology; this covers the terms and abbreviations used in the various documents which accompany the software and for the identification of program files. It also includes the rules for assigning names to the various software procedures.

Software Production Methodology

Coding itself represents only one component of the software production process; it is equally necessary for every program to be consistent with all other programs (developed by other programmers). The latter aspect is particularly crucial at the software/hardware integration phase when the combination of assorted software produced by different programmers starts. At this stage of the product development process, any software inconsistencies will have technical and human consequences which are difficult to handle and serious for the project (see Chapter 6).

3.1 The Architecture of Module Organization

Every computing project contains a great deal of software which, for optimum production, must be divided into several parts in accordance with the amount of software to be realized in functional terms.

The starting point is partitioning of the software into subsections in accordance with the general architecture of the product, as it is with hardware.

3.1.1 Project Partitioning

The first stage in software production is partitioning of the project into subsections (see Fig. 3.3). Each subsection is assumed to correspond to a component of the project which provides a range of functions (examples are text processing, compatibility checking, communication, an operating system and so on). In some cases there is a software development team for each subsection.

3.1.2 Partitioning into Modules

Each subsection is broken down into distinct modules. The module is the basic element of the project software architecture. Each module is assumed to fulfil one

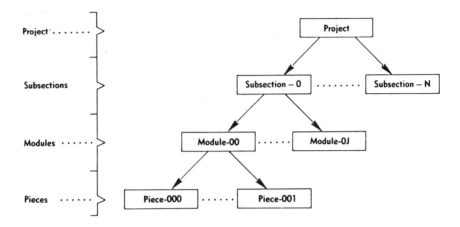

Figure 3.3 Partitioning a project to the level of basic 'pieces'.

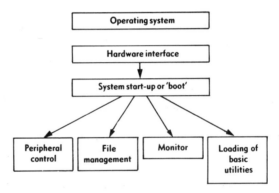

Figure 3.4 Division of the 'operating system' subsystem into modules.

function (see the example of Fig. 3.4). This decomposition must respect modularity as defined in structured programming; it will be treated later in this chapter.

3.1.3 A Piece of Code

A piece of code is the basic element of software production; it is the program file itself. In order to maintain control of the software, the complexity of the piece of code must be limited (its length should be less than about 100 instructions). A module generally consists of several pieces of code.

All the decompositions mentioned previously must be accompanied by a number of rules of dialogue between the various parts; these 'communication' elements are defined in the interface files (for the whole project, for subsections, for modules and for pieces of code). These files represent the 'contract' between programmers in different software development teams. These files contain the shared data together with the services (procedures) which the operating system provides on request. This contract must respect a defined structure (see page 42).

Examples are:

- A program 'GCOMP11A.PLM', written in PLM86, which requests the display of a string of characters; this service is performed by the procedure 'VIS-Paint-Txt'.
- An interface file 'VISP12.HED' which contains the declaration of the procedure 'VIS-Paint-Txt'. The name of the interface file must contain a reference to the module or subsection which offers the service. In this example, it is the display management module 'VIS'.
- The program 'GVISP11A.PLM' which contains the code which enables the service to operate.

Two approaches are possible when interfacing with files which contain the declarations of services which are available on request (the requests are generally from application software); either all available services are included in a single file which the requesting program includes in its file (see Fig. 3.5(b)), or each module

```
            .
$INCLUDE (:F2:VISP.HED)
            .
            .
            .
call VIS_Paint_Txt(@str,2);
            .
            .
            .
```

(a) GCOMP11A.PLM

```
            .
            .
VIS_Paint_Txt: procedure (ptxt, mode)
                              external;
        Declare ptxt Pointer;
        Declare mode Byte;
    end VIS_Paint_Txt;
```

(b) VISP12.HED

```
VIS_Paint_Txt: procedure (ptxt,mode) public reentrant;
    Declare ptxt Pointer
            (txt Based ptxt) (256) Byte;
    Declare (mode,I) Byte;

    do I=1 TO txt(0);
        call VIS_Paint_Car(Signed(txt(I)),mode);
    end;
    end VIS_Paint_Txt;
```

(c) GVISP11A.PLM

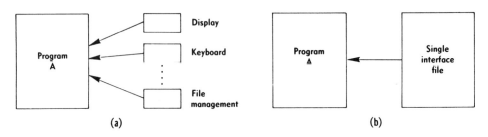

Figure 3.5 The use of interface files. (a) The interface files are separated according to service type. (b) A single interface file contains all the services.

offers a file which contains the available services which each application program can call, individually, in accordance with its requirements (see Fig. 3.5(a)).

3.1.4   Organization and Structure

Software is a structured entity of which the 'applications' part forms one layer (see Fig. 3.6). All the modules make use of the services contributed by the common system base, such as access to peripheral devices, in such a way as to avoid access conflicts in multitask operation and redundancy of development.

Applications operate by making calls to the procedure entry points which are available in the operating system. Some data internal to the system must be completely transparent to applications (examples are a file structure description table and updating of records during modification to a file). In any case, an application does not directly access the electronic hardware without passing through the operating system, particularly when the operating system operates in multitask mode. Some microprocessors provide protection of memory areas which are reserved exclusively for the operating system (see the section on memory management in Chapter 4). These areas are assigned to routines internal to the operating system or to confidential data.

The operating system of the product can be specific (its design may be subcontracted or developed internally), or standard (for example: MSDOS, UNIX, CP/M, ISIS, VersaDos etc.). In the case where the operating system is specific, it is desirable that its development should be accomplished within the organization. The real-time monitor, the operating system and the hardware interface module form the kernel of the software architecture.

The software/hardware interface (see Fig. 3.6), when correctly implemented, permits the architecture of the electronic hardware and this part of the interface to be changed without modifying other software. This module isolates all software above this layer (see Fig. 3.6) since this software sees the electronic hardware as an abstract machine which performs operations (these operations are no longer accessible on the packages themselves but at the hardware/software interface).

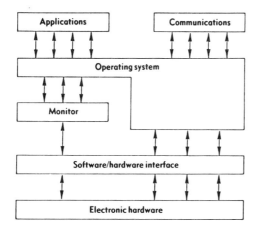

Figure 3.6 Architecture and organization of subsystems in a data-processing system.
   The hardware part represents all the programmable electronic components of the product.
   The real-time monitor section controls the tasks in the case of a multitask system. In general, all accesses to the hardware must pass through the monitor or operating system. The monitor is very closely involved with the operating system.
   The operating system controls the following:

– Start-up of the product when power is applied; this includes testing of electronic components, initialization of various peripherals and some software such as the monitor.
– File management (creation, deletion, copying etc.).
– Loading of basic utilities into the working memory.

All applications must have access to the various services available in the operating system by way of entry points which are available to applications (see the section on user documentation for computer specialists).

3.1.5   Ergonomic Aspects

The product will be much better received if account has been taken of ergonomic factors; this requires discussion and prior agreement between the groups involved. These factors are:

• Consistency in the use of the applications available in the product is imperative and agreement must be imposed on the various development groups. This includes the presentation of menus, the use of function keys, the form of messages etc.
• The various items which the user is required to manipulate must be easily accessible.
• The product is to be used in a working environment and the answers to questions such as the following should be readily accessible: 'How is it used?', 'What must be

done now?' 'How does one get back to the starting-point?' It is always difficult for these items to be analysed by someone from a purely computer technology point of view; the assistance of a third person with a knowledge of ergonomics is valuable.

- Different arrangements of the proposed message displays must be examined, for example separation of the information and error message display areas. The implications of the screen and keyboard configuration must be analysed.
- The messages must be clear.
- It must be possible to call up the user menu(s) at any time when using the various applications.
- The response times must be reasonable.
- The form of the product must not lead to rejection by the user but should be attractive to him or her (this aspect is associated with the aesthetics of design).
- The location of certain keys must be such as to avoid operational errors. Examples are: (1) The 'EXECUTE' and 'CANCEL' buttons should not be too close to each other or to other non-functional buttons. (2) The 'RESET' button should be difficult for the user to access (although it must normally be provided).

Difficulties arise if the product has fast response times and powerful functions coupled with an awkward mode of use which can be learned only slowly by a non-computer specialist.

The ideal in the use of any tool is to concentrate the user's attention on the task to be achieved and not on the use of the tool itself.

3.1.6 Adaptation to International Markets

It is often desirable that a microprocessor-based product which is under development should be available in the various configurations which enable it to be adapted to the requirements of the international market.

Adaptation for the international market poses four types of problem as follows:

- The character set should be suitable for each country.
- The messages displayed on the screen must be in the language of the country.
- Writing is from left to right or vice versa as appropriate; in some cases both directions of writing must coexist (this also involves cursor displacement).
- The keyboard configuration must be to the standard of each country or group of countries.

To facilitate adaptation, it is desirable that:

- Character style definition should be stored in a software module and not read only memory; the latter makes it slow and difficult to modify characters or to add new ones which are not in the ASCII or EBCDIC sets. The read/write memory area available for storing these characters must be sufficiently large to support the maximum number of characters required, particularly for countries which use two or more different languages or a large number of characters (the form of the characters in some countries requires high resolution in the character-defining matrix). A utility for loading the characters into peripherals, such as printers, should also be provided.

- Messages visible to the user (such as error messages, lists of utilities and commands etc.) should be in a separate software module; the version for each language can then be loaded as required.
- The part containing the basic utilities should be accessible to a computer specialist.
- The screen cursor management section should also be in a module (for access to the direction of cursor displacement during writing).
- The assignment of characters to keyboard keys should be capable of modification; possibly by the availability of a character assignment utility for the keys.

The availability of the above modules provides the possibility of modification without difficulty by a computer specialist; message length parameters should also be accessible.

3.2   Software Documentation

Software documentation is as important as the coding itself; the availability of this documentation is fundamental in a computing project.

3.2.1   Introduction

Substantial effort should be devoted to software documentation before the coding itself (see Fig. 3.2). This documentation facilitates the following:

- Verification of the consistency of programs with the functional specifications and general architecture (inconsistency is a source of errors in the final product creation phase when modules and subsections are combined in the software/hardware integration phase). Logical errors in the solutions adopted to perform the required product functions can be made evident before any program writing. All these aspects reduce the number of logical errors before program production.
- Control of maintenance and minimization of the consequences of turnover of development personnel.
- Reduction of the cost of the software/hardware integration phase.
- Successful development in every phase of production including manufacturing and subsequent development of the product.

Various types of software documentation, directly associated with software production, will be required as follows:

- 'Organic' documentation – definitions of the functions to be realized.

- Analytical documentation – definitions of the logical solution(s) for execution of the required function(s).
- Unit and global test documentation – lists of tests to be performed individually on the software.
- Software/hardware integration documentation – checks for consistency with the general specifications.

From the start of development, a clear and precise definition should be provided for the contents of each type of document to be produced. In general, the majority of the errors discovered during testing and maintenance are errors of specification or design (caused by lack of documentation, poor organization in the production of the documentation or lack of respect for the documentation rules). The cost of correcting these errors increases in proportion to the elapsed time from the first unit tests. The objective is to be able to test the specifications before the design stage and the design before the realization phase.

3.2.2   The Organic Specification Document

Based on the general architecture documentation (see Chapter 2), the organic specification document contains a description of the methods (in purely data-processing terms) used to realize the required functions; this documentation contains:

- The choice of method for function realization.
- The structure of the files used (their organization, structure and format).
- A list of interfaces with other subsections.
- Partitioning into modules.
- The functions of each module and the interactions between modules which are either internal or external to subsections.
- Data, either internal or external to modules and subsections, which are shared and data which are available to subsections.
- The conditions under which processing is activated; activation conditions which are internal and external to subsections should be separated.
- Special cases such as fast response times (the acceptable limits must be defined).
- The operating conditions in the case of a multitasking system (a list of tasks, priorities, time required for different tasks, a list of critical resources etc.).

Each subsection must have at least one organic specification document.

3.2.3 The Analysis Document

In this documentation, each module is analysed in detail before proceeding to programming. All pieces of code, such as those described previously, are listed. This documentation must contain a general description of the module, the processing to be performed by each piece of code and a detailed description of the procedures contained in the pieces of code.

The module description contains:

- The module name.
- The module functions.
- A list of the pieces of code and the processing performed by each one.
- Shared data which are either internal or external to the module.
- A description of all variables with distinction between those internal and those external to the module.
- A flow diagram in structured programming form.
- A list of the services required of other subsections together with those available for the subsections.
- A description of each procedure contained in the various pieces of code with distinction between internal procedures and public procedures for the subsection and for the whole project.

The procedures are described in pseudocode such as program design language (PDL); this language is similar to natural language, but a number of rules for key words and characters (see Tables 3.1 and 3.2) must be observed.

Example of a procedure analysis.

```
Open_FileAP: Procedure (^Name_file, ^error);
        {variable initialization}
File_open      ← false           {not yet open}
Name_file      ← Name_file_sys {insert the name of the file to be opened}
Error          ← false

        {request file opening}
SGF_Open_File (^Name_file, mode=R/W, ^error_SGF)
if error_SGF <> 0 then

        {error in opening of file}
        do
            error ← error_SGF
            return
        end
            {correct opening}
            .
            .
            .
```

Table 3.1   Keywords of the analysis document.

DO
   Action 1
   END
IF condition
     THEN Action 1
     ELSE Action 2
ENDIF
WHILE Condition
    Repeated action
END
UNTIL Condition
    Repeated action
END
FOR Condition.
    Repeated action
END
SELECT Criterion
   WHEN Value 1
         Action 1
   WHEN Value 2
         Action 2
   OTHER Value i
         Action i
END
EXIT
EXITIF
RETURN

Table 3.2   Key characters of the analysis document.

Key characters	Significance
{ }	Comment
←	Assignment
AND	Logical AND
OR	Logical OR
= <> <= >=	Logical condition test
∧	Pointer

3.2.4   The Unit Test Document

This is the preparatory document for unit testing; the objective of these unit tests is to confirm that execution of the code conforms to the items contained in the analysis document. Each procedure is tested individually. This documentation will serve as a guide to all the tests to be performed on the software. When the tests have been completed, the unit and global test documentation containing all the results of the tests performed is sent to the software/hardware integration team.

Each piece of code, as defined previously, must have its unit test documentation. In the testing phase, each instruction of a piece of code must be executed at least once. The constraints due to 'real time' aspects are ignored at this stage of testing.

The unit test documentation must contain the following information:

● The testing tools – the development system, software listings etc.
● The test conditions – the tools used, the nature of the tests and the operating frequency.
● The procedures to be tested.
● The results expected of the procedures for each test, in terms of the specification of each procedure.
● The test data.

3.2.5   The Global Test Document

The objective of the global tests or static functional tests is to verify the conformity of all functions taken individually with the organic specification documentation. As for the unit test documentation, the documentation to prepare for the global tests of a module will be produced after the validation phase of the module analysis document.

The global test documentation is very similar to that of the unit tests but it must contain the functions and not the procedures taken individually (a function is, in general, a series of procedures, see Fig. 3.7). During the software tests, all functions must be tested including limiting cases (see marginal effects, Chapter 5). Each module and each subsection must have global test documentation.

All unit and global tests are static; dynamic tests correspond to software and hardware testing in the actual operating environment (aspects such as real-time

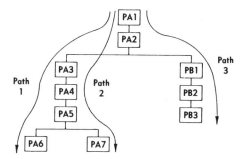

Figure 3.7 Function execution by calling procedures. Several paths are possible according to the state of the data evaluated in the function execution process. All these paths which are defined and associated with the function must be tested.

operation and the environment in which the product is required to operate must be taken into account). Dynamic tests are performed at the end of the software/ hardware integration phase and in the product qualification phase (see Chapter 5).

3.2.6   Software/Hardware Integration Document

The software/hardware documentation is written from the first stages of development of the product; its objective is to verify the consistency of the various software subsections, the software/hardware consistency and the conformity of all programs and hardware to the general product specification. This paves the way for tests which locate all global operational errors. This documentation must contain:

- The nature of the tests with details of the tools used, the items to be tested and so on.
- A list of the functions to be tested.
- The expected results of the tests.
- A list of the modules and subsections to be tested.

Once the integration team receives the software and the prototype, the next step is to check the software/hardware integration documentation as follows.

The various pieces of code, which have previously been tested, are combined to form the subsections of the product. The 'real time' aspects will be tested at this stage and the response times of functions will be evaluated. This will bring to light timing problems associated with slow execution times, the time taken to access the central processing unit, synchronization and so on. The software/hardware integration documentation will be concluded with the results obtained in the various tests.

Note   In addition to the tests themselves, the following two aspects must be taken into account and defined from the first stages of coding:

- The assignment of memory addresses, if necessary, to the software (see Fig. 3.8). This assignment enables overlapping of software to be avoided, particularly in the integration phase, and the volume of software to be limited to a certain extent.

- Consistency in the options selected during generation of executable files (consistency in the compilation options, the parameters of the linking editor etc.).

3.3   Choice of Programming Languages

In designing the various pieces of code, the choice of language depends on the function of the program. Two types of language are used in writing code for the software of a computer project; these are assembly languages and high-level languages (Pascal, Ada, C etc.).

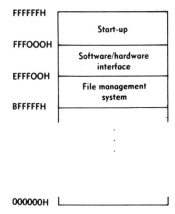

Figure 3.8 Physical location of modules in memory at the development stage.

The choice of high-level language is an equally important factor in the design process. In addition to the availability, or otherwise, within the organization of experience of one or more high-level languages, the choice is determined by the requirements and particular features of the software (see Table 3.5).

3.3.1 Assembly Language

A program written in assembler is a series of lines of symbolic instructions; a utility (an assembler) permits conversion of the source program into an object program (in binary format). During this conversion each instruction line is replaced by its equivalent in binary code (machine language); the latter code is directly recognized by the microprocessor.

An instruction written in assembler consists of the following (see Fig. 3.9):

- A label field.
- A code field.
- An operand field.
- A comment field.

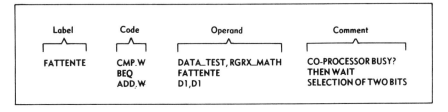

Figure 3.9 The component parts of an instruction written in assembler.

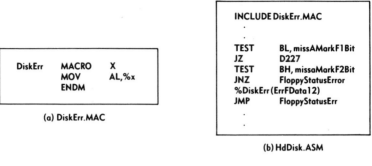

(a) DiskErr.MAC

(b) HdDisk.ASM

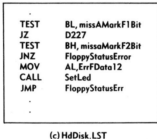

(c) HdDisk.LST

Figure 3.10 Definition and use of a macro-instruction: (a) DiskErr.MAC – definition of the macro-instruction 'DiskErr' containing the formal argument x; this macro illuminates the error LEDs on the disk drive card (see Chapter 3); (b) the assembler source program 'HdDisk.ASM' calling the macro-instruction 'DiskErr' with the real argument 'ErrFData12'; (c) HaDisk.LST – the list file of the assembler program 'HdDisk.ASM'.

The advantages of a program written in assembler are as follows:

- Speed of execution.
- The small amount of memory space required.
- Parameterization of values (the length of tables, assignment of input/output ports).
- The closeness of the language to language directly recognized by the microprocessor; this permits maximum utilization of the hardware facilities, particularly at microprocessor level.
- The availability of macro-instructions which permit substitution of text. This substitution is made during assembly of the source program; it also includes the replacement of arguments. The availability of these macro-instructions permits simplification and clarity in the maintenance of programs written in assembler (see Fig. 3.10, Table 3.3 and Table 3.4 for the operators).

Table 3.3   List of the most common assembler macros.

Designation	Function
MACRO/ENDM	Definition of a macro (see Fig. 3.10)
IF THEN ELSE	Conditional assembly (see Fig. 3.12)
ENDIF	End of a conditional macro (see Fig. 3.12)
WHILE	Conditional assembly for a number of times determined by a parameter (see Fig. 3.13).
REPEAT	Permits an instruction to be repeated for a number of times defined by the contents of the parameter REPEAT (see Fig. 3.14).
OUT	Message display during assembly. (For example, a display on the screen of the message 'Assembly of the RAM test section' %OUT Assembly of the RAM test section.)
RADIX	Initialization of the bases of numerical expressions. B for binary, D for decimal, H for integer hexadecimal, O for octal and R for real hexadecimal.

Table 3.4   List of the most common assembler operators (macros).

Designation	Function
§	An operator which permits parameterization of an argument (see the parameter MSG§COUNT of Fig. 3.11).
=	An operator which permits a numerical expression to be assigned to a variable (for example, COUNT = 4).
%	The calling operator for a macro-instruction (see Fig. 3.10).

The disadvantages are:

- The cost of development is relatively high.
- Productivity is generally low.
- Maintenance is difficult, particularly for large programs (greater than 1000 lines).
- Expertise and experience of the language are required of the programmer. In the majority of cases, the operation and internal architecture of the microprocessor which supports the assembly language must be known perfectly. This requires a substantial period of learning.
- The difficulty in keeping track of programs and monitoring them (for example reading by another programmer).
- Portability is restricted solely to microprocessors using the same language (for example, an assembler program written for the 80386 microprocessor would have to be entirely rewritten if it were to be reused on an MC 68020 microprocessor).

```
MSGERR      MACRO          TEXT
            CNTR=CNTR+1
            %MSG (CNTR, TEXT)
            ENDM

;
MSG         MACRO          COUNT, CHARACTERS
MSG§COUNT   DB        CHARACTERS
            ENDM
```

Figure 3.11 Overlapping of two macros. The parameter MSGCOUNT is dependent on the value of COUNT. For example, if COUNT = 1, the parameter MSG§COUNT becomes MSG1).

```
IF COUNT GT 0 THEN
OUT 61,AL

;
ELSE
IN AL,60
ENDIF
```

Figure 3.12 A conditional macro. This permits generation of one of two types of code according to whether the condition is true or false.

```
; Reassembly as long as n is positive
%WHILE (N GT 0)
n=n−1
;
```

Figure 3.13 The use of a loop.

```
%REPEAT (4)
(       DB 0)
;
; is equivalent to
DB 0
DB 0
DB 0
DB 0
```

Figure 3.14 Repetition in writing an instruction.

Assembler language is preferable above all when there are constraints such as:

- Access to electronic packages and internal microprocessor registers by the source program.
- Execution times.
- Available memory space.

3.3.2   High-level Languages

High-level languages have been designed with instructions expressed sufficiently simply (similarly to human language) for programs to be designed, understood and modified easily.

As with a program written in assembler language, the source program written in a high-level language must be translated into machine language. This operation is performed by the compiler: each high-level language, of course, has it own compiler and its own particular features (see Table 3.5).

Table 3.5   Some high-level languages.

Language	Features
Pascal	Derived from ALGOL, the Pascal language was defined by Niklaus Wirth in 1970. It is suitable for structured programming.
Ada	Defined by J. Ichbiach, the American Defense Department retained this language in 1979 as a universal programming language. It is suitable for both application and basic software.
C	Developed by Dennis Ritchie of Bell Telephone Laboratories, the C language has the advantage that compact programs can be written. This is particularly appreciated for basic software.
FORTRAN	FORTRAN was one of the first scientific languages.
COBOL	A language devoted to management programs.
Occam	A language developed by the INMOS company. Occam is suitable for processing several processes simultaneously and in controlling processors of the *transputer* type.

The advantages of a program written in a high-level language are as follows:

- The development cost is relatively low.
- Follow-up and monitoring of source programs is better.
- The readability of the instructions permits self-documentation of the source program.
- Maintenance is facilitated.
- The programs are portable to other types of product and other microprocessors.

The disadvantages are:

- The speed of execution is slow in comparison with assembler.
- More memory space is required. A program written in a high-level language generally includes more instructions when compiled than if it had been written directly in assembly language.

3.3.3   The Assembler/High-level Language Interface

Quite often a large part of the software is written in a high-level language (such as Pascal, C and Ada); however, some parts may require to be written in assembler on account of constraints such as those associated with speed and memory capacity limitations. The links between the two types of software are provided by the linkage editor utility (see Chapter 5).

To establish a link and pass parameters correctly between two types of language, it is necessary to observe the conventions for generating code from a high-level language during compilation. This is because each type of high-level language has its own particular approach to handling the microprocessor registers, the passing of parameters and the return of processed data to the initiator. The assembler must, therefore, respect the conventions of the high-level language with which it coexists.

In general, the registers must be restored with the same contents when control is returned to the caller of a procedure (for example, in the case of the 8086 these are the code-segment (CS), stack-segment (SS), stack-pointer (SP), base-pointer (BP) and data-segment (DS) registers).

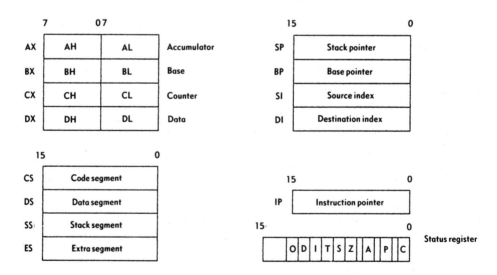

Figure 3.15 The internal registers of the 8086.

```
                    .
                    .
                    .
; Up-date the parameter stack

    MOV AX, SEG val
    PUSH AX

                    .
                    .
; Procedure call

    CALL CONV_VAL
    ; Recovery of parameters stored on the stack
    ADD   SP,10
    ;Recovery of return data stored in AX
    MOV WORD PTR valr, AX

                    .
                    .
                    .
```

Figure 3.16 Calling a procedure in a high-level language from an assembler program.

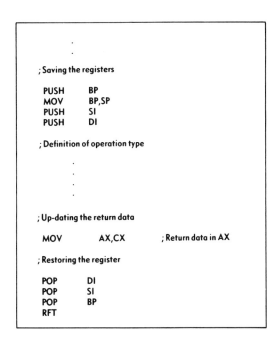

```
                    .
                    .
; Saving the registers

    PUSH      BP
    MOV       BP,SP
    PUSH      SI
    PUSH      DI

; Definition of operation type

                    .
                    .
                    .
                    .

; Up-dating the return data

    MOV           AX,CX          ; Return data in AX

; Restoring the register

    POP       DI
    POP       SI
    POP       BP
    RFT
```

Figure 3.17 An example of an assembler procedure which can be called by a high-level language (the C language).

During the calling of a procedure defined in a high-level language from the assembler (the 8086 assembler is taken as an example in this section), it is necessary, at assembler program level (see Fig. 3.16), to start by saving the various current parameters on the stack (the current parameters must be saved in the order in which the high-level language saves its own current parameters) together with certain registers (CS, SS, SP, BP and DS – see Fig. 3.15). When the assembler calls a procedure defined in a high-level language, saving of the registers is not always obligatory (see Fig. 3.16) since high-level languages save the registers on compilation and restore them at the end of execution (see Fig. 3.17).

The return data are generally sent to the caller either in register AL if it is a byte, in register AX if it is a short integer (16 bits) or in DX:AX or AX:BX for the other types of data (long integers and pointers).

The assembler program must reset the stack pointer (SP) to its initial value before the initial saving and restore the contents of the saved registers (DS, SS and BP) before returning control to the high-level language (see Fig. 3.17).

Note   In certain cases, there are differences, even in the same high-level language, in the handling of internal registers. These are originally associated with the designer of the high-level language, the version or the type of option used during compilation of the source program (for example, SMALL, MEDIUM, LARGE).

3.4   Structured Programming

3.4.1   Introduction

Founded on the mathematical basis of Bohm and Jacopini, structured programming has the following facilities:

- Good legibility. Reading from left to right and top to bottom enables the execution of each module to be easily assimilated, thereby facilitating comprehension of programs.
- Easy communication. This enables any programmer to take over programs written by others and facilitates communication between programmers.
- Better software maintenance. The interactions between different programs are clearly identified; this enables incidents due to software development to be isolated both in the general architecture and in the aspects internal to the program itself.
- Reuse of software. Since the function and position in the general structure are clearly identified, the portability of software to other projects is facilitated.

By using structured programming, subroutines can be produced which can be called by different modules each time the particular service is required. This enables the developer to limit the length of his software and to manage it better by using a modular system (this facilitates maintenance, portability, testing and modification).

A structured system consists of a set of modules; each module fulfils one function and has a single input and a single output. Processing observes the 'top-down' concept, which involves decomposition of the flow diagram into a tree-like structure. The flow diagram is written and read from left to right and top to bottom.

The 'GOTO' instruction gives rise to several exit points from modules; consequently it is eliminated from programs, particularly as every 'GOTO' instruction can be replaced by other instructions which respect the rules of structured programming.

Global data must also be structured since they can be accessed by several modules and must retain correct accessibility. When a data error arises, it is often difficult to isolate the procedure which generates this error since several procedures share the same data (see Fig. 3.18).

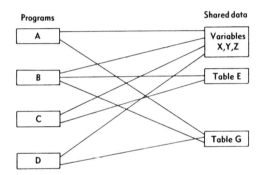

Figure 3.18 A poor shared data structure increases debugging and software maintenance costs.

The objective is to limit the amount of shared data as far as possible (the passing of parameters between procedures is recommended in order to limit the amount of shared data to an absolute minimum). The remaining shared data should be organized into levels as follows:

- Shared data reserved for modules.
- Shared data reserved for subsections.
- Shared data reserved for the whole project.

3.4.2 Control Structures

To analyse a given problem, structured programming uses three control structures. Every algorithm can be expressed by means of these, which are as follows:

- BLOCK
- IFTHENELSE
- DOWHILE (and/or DOUNTIL).

A BLOCK or 'process' represents an instruction or sequence of instructions which enables data to be modified. A block has one input and one output. A block can be a subprogram with a single entry point (see Fig. 3.19); it can also be a succession of two or more blocks.

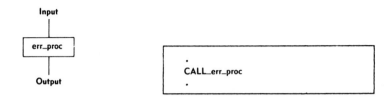

Figure 3.19 The subroutine 'Err-proc'; the function of this subroutine is to display an error message (the output) as a function of the error number (the input).

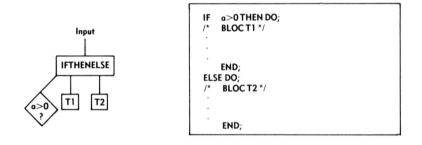

Figure 3.20 If the condition is true, execute block T1, otherwise execute T2.

IFTHENELSE represents a condition (see Fig. 3.20). One output or the other is taken according to the state of the data tested (a form of branching).

CASEOF is similar to IFTHENELSE but offers the choice of one output from several (multiple branching – see Fig. 3.21).

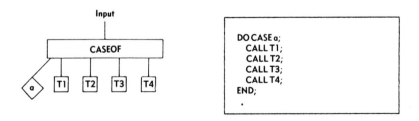

Figure 3.21 Generalization of IFTHENELSE.

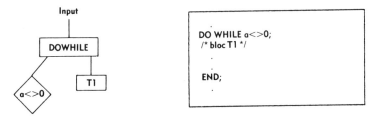

Figure 3.22 A loop; as long as the condition is true, block T1 is executed.

DOWHILE (and DOUNTIL) represents a loop (see Fig. 3.22). A 'BLOCK' is executed as long as, or until, the condition is true.

3.4.3 Functional Decomposition

Analysis of a problem leads to functional decomposition which can be represented in the form of a tree which starts from the top and leads to the separate functions at the bottom as shown in Fig. 3.23. This representation permits subtrees, which represent the programs to execute each function, to be isolated. Each subtree can be given a meaningful name, corresponding to the function performed, such as 'start-warm' and 'start-cold'. This approach can enable all the required operations for each program to be set out on a single sheet; the interactions with the module or

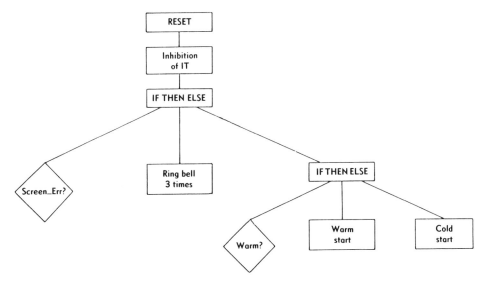

Figure 3.23 Simplified 'bootstrap' start-up module of a product. Two types of start-up are possible: a cold start which corresponds to the first application of power to the product, and a warm start which corresponds to a restart under power.

subsection architecture and the constraints associated with realization and use can also be included. The self-consistent sections which have a characteristic function common to several trees can be identified and isolated in the form of services which can be called from any module. These sections can, in certain cases, limit the overall length of the software and consequently reduce the duration of software testing and the maintenance costs. An example of functional decomposition is the start-up routine or 'bootstrap' of a product.

When power is applied the 'RESET' signal is activated and the address vectors correspond to a call to the start-up module. The start-up module generally performs the following operations (see Fig. 3.23):

- Inhibition of interrupts.
- Display testing – if display operation is not correct, bleep three times and stop the system.
- Warm or cold start testing. The test is made by means of a status register which is specific to the system and a check value which is stored in RAM; these two values are stored in battery-backed RAM, supported by the product power supply if it has a stand-by mode or in EEPROM if these are used. The values are updated when the product is first powered up (a cold start).

The two types of start follow from the diagram of Fig. 3.23 (warm – see Fig. 3.24; cold – see Fig. 3.25).

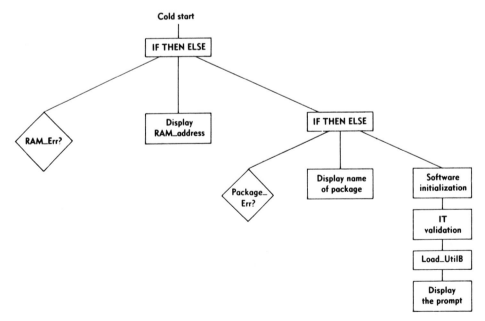

Figure 3.24 Detailed sections of a warm start.

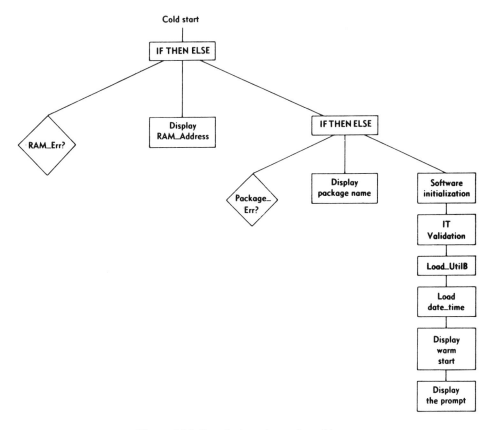

Figure 3.25 Detailed sections of a cold start.

A warm start includes the following:

- RAM test – if a RAM is defective, display the address of the defective device and stop the system.
- Test and initialization of programmable electronic devices and peripherals (other than the display) – if a device or peripheral is defective, display the name and stop the system.
- Software initialization, if required (such as resetting the various queues to zero).
- Interrupt checking.
- Loading of basic operating system utilities into memory.
- Displaying the 'prompt' message and passing control to the user.

A cold start includes the following:

- RAM test – if a RAM is defective, display the address of the defective device and stop the system.

- Test and initialization of programmable electronic devices and peripherals (other than the display) – if a device or peripheral is defective, display the name and stop the system.
- Software initialization, if required (such as resetting the various queues to zero).
- Interrupt checking.
- Setting the control register.
- Loading of basic operating system utilities into memory.
- Loading the date and time.
- Loading the value to indicate a warm start.
- Displaying the 'prompt' message and passing control to the user.

3.5 File Organization

3.5.1 Program Names

A methodology for organizing the various program files enables time to be saved in the development process and in the various inter-departmental transfers which arise when the project requires substantial interaction of the development teams.

This methodology applies both to the various aspects of the structure and organization of a program file and also to the visible aspects such as the name and the various indices (see Fig. 3.26) which enable the stages of evolution to be identified during software development and in the keeping of records.

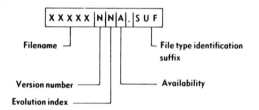

Figure 3.26 The various parts of a program name.

Filenames

The name must suggest the significance and role of the file in the project as a whole. Examples are:

- UAFMS, user access to file management system
- TRLP, transport layer program.

Note In some cases it is necessary to distinguish files which have the same name but use different programming languages. Examples are:

- UAFMSP, a program in the Pascal language
- UAFMSA, a program in assembly language.

The version

The version number enables the versions available to the various users and the functions contained within the software to be made to correspond (version management). The value is incremented by one for every modification, whether functions are added or removed, and when the hardware configuration is modified.

The development index

The index number corresponds to the updates of the source file; this index is incremented for developments associated with the software design (correction of errors following testing, software performance improvements and so on). The index number is not in any way concerned with changes in the specification (specification changes correspond to the version number).

Note The set of documentation associated with a piece of software must always be updated during every change of the index or version of the software. In this way a constant link is maintained between the software and the documents associated with it.

Availability

The availability of the module is identified by a letter (A, B or C); each of these letters provides information on the state of development of the software. This index is strictly internal to development personnel. Examples are:

UAFMS11A, a program in course of development.
UAFMS11B, a program in the software/hardware integration phase.
UAFMS11C, a program available for qualification.

The suffix

The suffix enables the file format (such as source, list, object etc.) to be identified. Examples are:

UAFMS11A.PAS, a source file in the Pascal language.
UAFMS11A.ASM, a source file in assembly language.
UAFMS11A.LST, a list file (the result of a compilation).
UAFMS11A.OBJ, an object file.

3.5.2 Internal File Organization

The internal structure of a source program is generally of the form shown in Fig. 3.27.

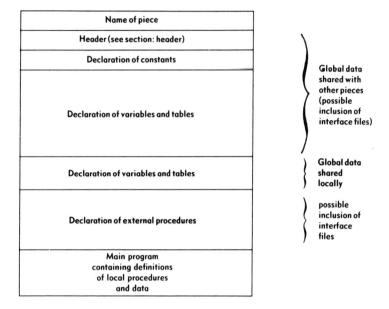

Figure 3.27 A program file generally contains the following:

- The filename.
- The header (see below).
- Constant declarations.
- Variable declarations.
- Network and table declarations.
- Declarations of external procedures and procedures included in interface files before coding of the procedures defined in the file. The data names must be significant.

The header

The following are listed in the file header in the form of comments:

- The filename.
- The function of the program.
- The initials of the program designer and the date of origination of the program.
- A development history of the various updates of the file; for each modification of the development index and version number, the date of the modification, the initials of the person responsible for the modification and the object of the modification are included in the file header.
- The list of public procedures contained in the program and the function of each of these procedures.
- Comments on the use of these public procedures.
- The name of the file should be included in the case of calls to these procedures.

An example of a source program header follows.

```
/**Filename: ESVID.PLM
**
**   Provides the video interface for 'stand-alone' diagnostics
**
**   Creation date: 17/06/83 by H.R.
**
**   Modifications:
**   -22/07/83 H.R. procedure Handler_ES transferred into module DIAES.PLM
**   -23/07/83 H.R. variables IO_DataTX added as externals
**   -07/08/83 H.R. modification to the procedure Vis_Moustiq
**   -10/10/83 D.S. *  slower display time t_delay+54,
                   *  modification to the prompt,
                   *  variable error_kbd added to the procedure Hd_errors
**   _
**
**   List of the public procedures contained in this module:
**       -VIS_RAZ_Screen,
**       -VIS_Display_car,
**       -VIS_Position_Cur,
**       -VIS_Determ_PCursor,
**
**   Comments:  before any call to the above procedures, the procedure
                VIS_Init_ES must be called.
**
**   For every call to the above procedures, the file Vid_Hand.HED must be included;
                this contains the procedure declarations and the various
                parameters required by these procedures.
**
  */
```

Procedure names

The name must be significant and relate to the function of the procedure. Several companies identify the names of procedures by a verb and the name of the object to which the action relates. For example, the procedure Read-Record corresponds to a procedure for reading a record in the context of a file management system.

Note In the case where this procedure can be called by other modules or subsections, an identifier of the original subsection can be assigned to it; this signifies the origin of the module and at the same time its availability to be called by a request for the service which it provides. For example, the procedure FMS-Read-File must be declared public and can be called by an application program to read the contents of a file.

Procedure information

This information is found either within the body of the procedure immediately after the name, or outside it immediately before the procedure declaration. This information (in the form of comments) includes the following:

- The function of the procedure.
- The name of the input and output parameters associated with the function and the role of each of these parameters.

An example of procedure information follows:

```
/*  Procedure KEYB_Light_LED (NLED,FUN);
**  Function: turn on and off the LEDs of the keyboard keys provided with LEDs.
**
**  Parameters:
**          NLED: identifier of the LED to be turned on or off.
**              NLED        Key
**              0           F10
**              1           F9
**              2           F8
**              3           F4
**              4           F3
**              5           F2
**              6           F1
**              7           LOCK
**              8           NUM
**          FUN: True – lit, False extinguished
**
*/
```

Note In certain cases of interdependence of programs a 'skeleton' can be used which enables development to continue unimpeded. A skeleton is a piece of software (a piece of code, a module or a subsection) which contains all the interface procedures called by the various application software. These procedures are empty (they do not contain the code necessary for execution of the requested service) but do permit the various development teams to interface with the empty services (a library of empty services). These services progressively become available from the development team; an example is development of a specific operating system by the software team.

Listing control parameters

The control parameters serve to facilitate the presentation and readability of the listings. These are the control words (see Table 3.6) which will be interpreted by the compiler while it generates the listing file.

Table 3.6 The most common listing control words.

Control word	Action
TITLE	Assignment of a title to the start of each page.
	Example: TITLE ('Screen management program')
PAGELENGTH	Specifies the number of lines per page.
	Example: PAGELENGTH (60) generates a listing with pages of
	60 lines.
PAGEWIDTH	Specifies the number of characters per line.
	Example: PAGEWIDTH (120) generates 120 characters per
	line.
EJECT	Indicates the end of the page and a jump to the following page.

3.6 Validation

To obtain quality software, checking and validation procedures must be performed at each stage. This includes documentation, coding, unit testing, global testing, integration and qualification. The desired actions are as follows:

* Re-reading of the documentation as well as the programs (static analysis). Re-reading of the code is achieved by exchanging programs between computer personnel; the objective is:

  ★ To detect logical errors.
  ★ To verify the program standards.
  ★ To locate structural faults.
  ★ To verify the technical feasibility.
  ★ To locate any inconsistencies with respect to the documentation.

  The documentation associated with the program is, in general, reviewed and validated by the project manager and the development team managers before program coding is started.
* Monitoring is performed by the development team managers for all the modules for which they are responsible.
* Audits by parties internal and external to the organization (those involved in the audit are not from the personnel directly participating in the product development).
* Validation by groups (the project manager and the development team managers).

  This validation has the following objectives:

* Observation of production standards (of documentation, code, testing procedures etc.).
* Consistency between the various components of a software module (documentation, code, testing).

- Technical feasibility. All the constraints (length, execution time, information rate, programming languages etc.) must be observed with a sufficient margin of safety.
- Consistency with other activities if there is interdependence.
- Consistency with the electronic hardware (addresses, device control etc.).
- Consistency with the overall specifications of the subsection and the whole project.

3.7 Qualification

A team independent of that realizing the product is required to qualify it; this qualification consists of verifying:

- Conformity of the product to the project specification (in terms of function, performance etc.).
- The reliability of the product.
- The man/machine dialogue procedures.
- Protection of work in progress in case of breakdown (for example, protection of work in progress during a power failure – see Section 4.17.1).
- The ease of operating the product.
- The limiting cases of operation (the maximum execution of work in a given time).
- The response times of the various functions.
- The quality and quantity of documentation.

All this work must be performed in the actual environment (typical and worst cases) where the product is required to operate. This service may also provide advice which improves production methods.

User Documentation for Computer Non-specialists and specialists

In the production of software, two sets of user documentation must generally be produced in collaboration with the commercial department; these two sets of documentation are dealt with in Sections 3.8 and 3.9.

3.8   User Documentation for Computer Non-specialists

This documentation is addressed to users who are not computer specialists. Its quality will determine whether its reader uses the product or not. Attractive presentation and simplicity of reading in addition to complete and comprehensible information are the factors to be taken into account.

First impressions are decisive; a poor impression at this stage is a serious disadvantage to the product. Good documentation, when properly done, is the 'finishing touch' which increases the likelihood of frequent sales and use. These first impressions are influenced by:

• The external appearance (the choice of packaging).
• The form and type of paper and cover.
• The type, form, length and arrangement of the various characters on the cover.

The documentation must contain:

• Information which indicates the various procedures to be followed in order to operate the product and a description of the items directly accessible to the user (switches, connectors and so on).
• Information on each utility which indicates:

  ⋆ The role of the utility.
  ⋆ A list of commands with their significance.
  ⋆ A list of messages which can be seen on the screen, including error messages.
  ⋆ The operational limits.
  ⋆ Examples of the use of each command.

While producing this documentation, it is necessary to have the attitude of a teacher wishing to communicate information to users; the background of the user who will consult the document should be considered.

This documentation should be checked by:

• A programmer who checks that all functions are described and that their uses are correct.
• A non-computer specialist user who takes note of the required learning times and those parts which are difficult to understand. The drafting of the parts concerned is subsequently re-examined.

3.9 User Documentation for Computer Specialists

It is of prime importance to establish and deliver the program documentation (or interface documentation for application software). This will provide the necessary tools for generating applications, by engineers internal and external to the organization which designed the product. The greater the number of applications, the greater the likelihood of commercial success of the product.

An application program interfaces through many entry points by using software calls to procedures contained in the operating system or other utility. The link between the application software and the operating system or utility is made during editing of the links by calls to various libraries which contain system procedures called from the application software.

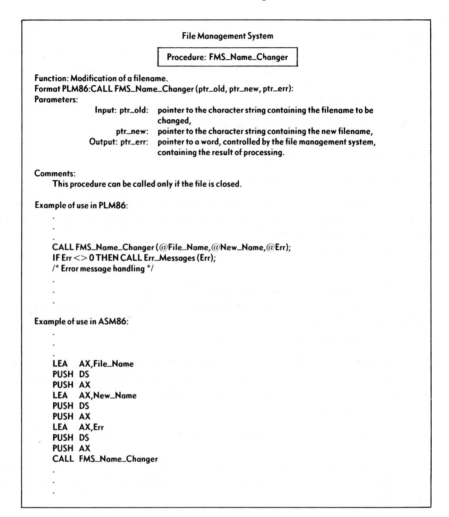

File Management System

Procedure: FMS_Name_Changer

Function: Modification of a filename.
Format PLM86:CALL FMS_Name_Changer (ptr_old, ptr_new, ptr_err):
Parameters:

Input: ptr_old: pointer to the character string containing the filename to be
                  changed,
ptr_new: pointer to the character string containing the new filename,
Output: ptr_err: pointer to a word, controlled by the file management system,
                   containing the result of processing.

Comments:
   This procedure can be called only if the file is closed.

Example of use in PLM86:

      .
      .

   CALL FMS_Name_Changer (@File_Name,@New_Name,@Err);
   IF Err <> 0 THEN CALL Err_Messages (Err);
   /* Error message handling */
      .
      .
      .

Example of use in ASM86:

      .
      .

   LEA   AX,File_Name
   PUSH DS
   PUSH AX
   LEA   AX,New_Name
   PUSH DS
   PUSH AX
   LEA   AX,Err
   PUSH DS
   PUSH AX
   CALL FMS_Name_Changer
      .
      .
      .

Figure 3.28 Description of the procedure FMS-Name Changer contained in the
program documentation.

This is user and development documentation for a computer specialist; consequently, this documentation lists all the system entry and exit points (the interfaces for application software – see Fig. 3.28). Each procedure or other form of entry point (for example a software interrupt) accessible by a user is listed; the information associated with the procedure and described in this documentation (see Fig. 3.28) is as follows:

• The name of the module containing the procedure.
• The name of the procedure.

- The function of the procedure.
- The calling format.
- The input and output parameters with the type and role of these parameters.
- Comments, such as the particular cases in which the procedure cannot be used or any other case of limited use.
- Examples of use in the different types of language which the computer specialist can use.
- In the header, the list of libraries containing the various procedures which the user can call from his application program.

The interface documentation for the application software will also contain the list of error messages for the modules containing procedures with error control arguments; these arguments are updated by the system. This list should preferably be at the end of a section describing the list of procedures for each module and not at the end of the document in an appendix.

It is desirable to add complete examples of the use of a module (such as an example containing the following operations: opening a file, insertion of data, removal of data and so on up to closure of the file (see Fig. 3.29)). These examples reflect the execution of a function by a call to several procedures (entry points) available in the operating system or in the various product utilities.

In certain cases, access to the services of one or more modules is made by observing a logical sequence before the services themselves are available; the attention of the reader will be drawn to the user documentation at the start of the module description section.

```
        :
mode = R/W                                                    /* Access mode */
sel_fil = FMS_create_file(@name,@err);                        /* File creation */
IF err <> 0 THEN CALL FMS_open_file(sel_fil,mode,@err);
ELSE CALL Abort_exit;                                         /* Problem in file creation */
        /* Insertion of text buffer characters into the file */
CALL FMS_insert_text(sel_fil,rank,@text,@err);


        .
        .
CALL FMS_release_file(sel_fil,@err);
        .
        .
        .
```

Figure 3.29 An example of the use of the file-management module.

Chapter 4

Hardware Development

Introduction

This chapter describes the design of the electronic hardware for a micro-processor-based product. The internal structure of the microprocessor will not be considered; it is assumed that at least an elementary description is familiar to the reader.

The aspects that will be considered in this chapter are associated with the design and use of the various components and the many requirements of a project which is based on one or more microprocessors. The various stages of hardware realization will also be considered.

At the start of hardware design (see section on Stages), the development managers generally have access to the following information:

- The type or types of microprocessor selected for the project.
- The approximate read/write memory (RAM) and read only memory (ROM) requirements.

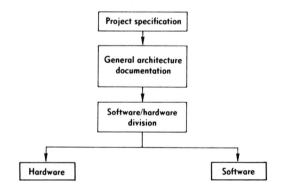

Figure 4.1 Location of the hardware design stage in the general development of the product.

- A list of requirements for hardware executable functions which can be utilized by the software (such as programmable chips, controllers, data converters, mathematical coprocessors and so on).
- The number and types of inputs and outputs.
- A list of the peripherals to be connected to the product.
- The required size and form of the product.
- The card dimensions.
- The location and physical space allocated to the power supply.

All this information has been defined (see Chapter 2) during software/hardware division (see Fig. 4.1).

Stages

Six principal stages are necessary (see Fig. 4.2) for the electronic hardware development section to produce one or more prototypes for delivery to the software/hardware integration section (see Chapter 5).

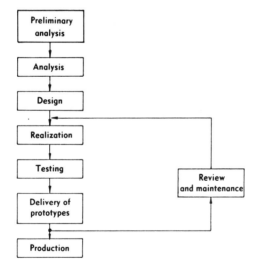

Figure 4.2 Stages in realizing the electronic hardware.

4.1   The Pre-design Stage

In this first stage, the hardware section defines the maximum number of cards (daughter boards) which the product can support on the basis of mechanical design information and also examines the mother board bus requirements (daughter and mother boards will be discussed later in this chapter).

To determine the maximum number of daughter boards which can be contained in the product, the useful length of the mother board (subtracting the length of the sections reserved for mounting and the power supply) is divided by the maximum distance separating two daughter boards.

Note The maximum number of cards is approximate, since some package heights require a greater inter-board separation than originally provided (see page 123).

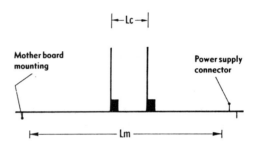

Figure 4.3 Defining the number of daughter boards and the mechanical feasibility of the product. $n = Lm/Lc$ where n is the number of daughter boards, Lm is the length of the mother board and Lc is the separation of the daughter boards or cards.

The width of the mother board can also be an important factor in the design of the product, particularly in connection with the type of bus which may be special or standard. In the case where the bus is standard, the cards have standardized lengths and widths which automatically influence the dimensions of the mother board. Buses will be discussed later in this chapter.

4.2 The Design Stage

According to the type of product and the information acquired during software/ hardware division (see Chapter 2) the hardware section embarks on the design stage which includes the following:

- Compilation of a list of all inputs and outputs with the characteristics of the signals required by each one and the number of LSI peripheral interface components to be used (if these have been selected). Any additional circuits required to adapt these signals to an industrial environment and permit compatibility of voltage and power levels, speed, etc. should also be noted.
- Definition of the memory map and the file which contains the access addresses to programmable devices such as controllers, peripheral interfaces, data converters,

multiplexers and so on; a significant name should be assigned to each address. This file can be used by the software section (the operating system development team – see Chapter 3) for access to the programmable electronic chips.

- Selection of components which meet the requirements of the functions to be realized as follows:

  ★ The LSI and VLSI components associated with the microprocessor and other supplementary devices (decoders, bus buffers, clock(s) etc.).
  ★ The types of read/write memory (static RAM, dynamic RAM or Application Specific Memory (ASM)), the memory capacity per chip and the access times (see page 81).
  ★ The types of read only memory EPROM or EPLD (required for realization of the prototype(s)) and the memory capacity per chip and the equivalent in PROM or ROM (required for the production phase); alternatively, devices of the PAL, PLA, PLD etc. type are becoming more and more widely used.
  ★ Special function components (mathematical coprocessors, hardware multiplier/dividers, analogue-to-digital and digital-to-analogue converters etc.).
  ★ Peripheral interface components (parallel, serial, hard and floppy disk drives, graphics controllers etc.).

- A decision on the type of bus (either special or standard) to be used on the mother board.
- Distribution of the various functions between cards. The total component area to be located on the card should be checked against the useful area available. Each individual function should be located on a single card if possible. This method permits later development; modification of one function involves modification of only one card.
- Definition of the system bus signals which will be available to the daughter boards. The signals necessary for extension and development of the product should be provided.
- Specification of the types of connector to be used on the cards and for connection with external standard and special peripherals. Selection of standard connectors for individual peripherals increases the range of possible commercial applications of the product.
- Determination of the total consumption of all components; this must be done for each required voltage.
- Determination of the power to be delivered at each voltage by the power supply unit.
- Examination of the case for protection against power failures. A period of maintained power should be provided in case of power failure (see page 120); this period determines the volume required for power storage components (i.e. capacitors).
- Decision on the actions to be taken in case of error or breakdown such as the provision of a 'watch-dog' (see page 121) and LED indicators for defective cards (see page 130).

- Decision on those elements which will and will not be powered in the case where the product has a stand-by mode.
- Examination of the feasibility of a power supply of adequate size.

4.3   The Detail Design Stage

At this stage, the various elements to be realized are examined, schematic diagrams are produced and the techniques which enable the functions to be fulfilled in electronic terms are chosen. This stage consists of:

- Production of schematic diagrams for the various cards which constitute the product.
- Definition of the interconnections between the various cards.
- Definition of the bus (standard or special) on the mother board.
- Definition of the significance of each signal and pin connection (signal identification) for all the connectors on the mother and daughter boards (see Fig. 4.4).
- Production of a schematic diagram of the power supplies.

Note   The assignment of connector pins to different signals on the various cards must, as far as possible, be identical for all connectors; this results in independence of the location of the cards on the mother board (see page 123).

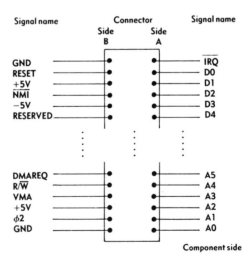

Figure 4.4 Identification of the signals on a mother board connector which are available to a daughter board.

4.4   The Realization Stage

This stage involves production of the various cards which make up the future product; it includes the processes discussed in Sections 4.4.1–3.

4.4.1   Schedule Creation

The schedule is an inventory of the various electronic components, connectors, transducers, mechanical components (such as motors) and so on which are required for the product. Each card must have its own schedule. Precise references for each active and passive component are specified in the schedule. These references must take account of the package type (dual in-line package (DIP), single in-line package (SIP), surface mounted, plastic, ceramic etc.) (see page 128) in order to define the area and mounting technique of the printed circuit.

4.4.2   Production of the Electronic Circuit Boards

Once the schematic diagrams and component schedules for each card have been defined, two modes of procedure are possible:

- Production of printed circuit boards (see page 125).
- Production of the boards by wire-wrapping. If very high-speed technologies (such as ECL) are used, wire-wrapping is not advised.

4.4.3 Power Supply Realization

Following definition of the various voltages required by the various components and calculation of the consumption at each of these voltages, the power supply is produced by the hardware section. Mechanical aspects and location must be taken into account.

4.5   The Testing Stage

When the electronic cards have been fabricated and the components inserted and soldered, the following stage is to test and validate each card and the power supply. The various card tests are detailed in the section on hardware tests in Chapter 5.

4.6   Follow-up and Maintenance

All the hardware, when tested (see Chapter 5), is delivered in the form of a prototype or prototypes to the software/hardware integration section (see Fig. 4.5); the latter

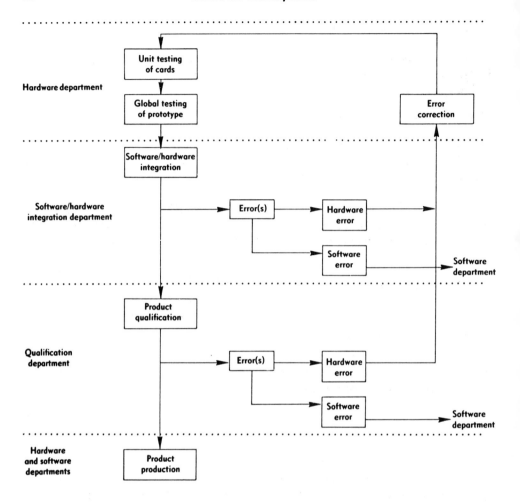

Figure 4.5 The testing and updating stages of the electronic hardware.

reports any electronic errors. The hardware design managers follow-up and analyse all these errors; the design section then makes the necessary modifications to both the hardware (using links and, ultimately, updating of the printed circuit) and the documentation. This follow-up is ensured by transfer to the qualification section (see Chapter 5).

When the hardware is completely tested and validated, the design section prepares for the manufacturing stage of the product; this includes:

- Updating of the manufacturing dossier.
- The introduction of modifications associated with manufacture (for example,

replacement of EPROMs by PROMs or ROMs according to the quantities to be produced, replacement of potentiometers, as far as possible, by fixed resistors etc.).

Basic Microprocessor System Components ————

A microprocessor-based system consists of one or more microprocessors; each microprocessor has access to read/write memory which permits temporary storage of data and code (a program loaded from hard or floppy disk), read only memory containing resident code (for example the start-up program), one or more clock circuits to generate the clock signals required by the various components and one or more peripheral interface devices. The last item provides a link with the external world which is directly accessible to the user by way of the peripherals.

After the various parts which make up a microprocessor-based product have been detailed, different types of interconnections and interfaces with peripherals will be given as examples.

4.7 Memory and Address Decoding

In accordance with the read/write and read only memory requirements, the technical specifications (constraints of speed, space, consumption etc.) and the commercial constraints (price), the hardware section defines the following:

- The type of memory chip to be used. This is governed by the required access time, power dissipated and storage capacity of each chip.
- The total read/write and read only memory capacities; a sufficient margin with respect to the preliminary requirements should be allowed (provide more than the actual capacity with empty space for memory packages on the memory board or boards in case large memory extensions which exceed the margin are required).
- The assignment of read/write and read only areas in the memory map. Memory chips are available in several configurations such as $2^n \times 1$ bits, $2^n \times 4$ bits, $2^n \times 8$ bits, $2^n \times 9$ bits, $2^n \times 16$ bits and so on.

4.7.1 Random Access Memory (RAM)

Random access memories (RAM) are volatile, that is the data are stored only as long as the power supply to the RAM is maintained as in the case of a microcomputer under power or RAM chips supplied from a battery.

For the design of the read/write memory section of the prototype, three types of RAM are available – dynamic RAM, static RAM and application specific memory (ASM).

Static RAM

Static RAM stores information in bistable flip-flops each of which forms the storage element for one bit. Static RAMs are of two types – slow SRAMs and fast SRAMs. The advantages of static RAM are as follows:

- A lower price for slow SRAMs.
- Ease of use.
- Low power consumption; this is one of the main advantages.

The disadvantages are:

- A low density of integration; this is the major disadvantage of SRAMs
- A high price for fast SRAMs.
- High power consumption by fast SRAMs.

The slow static RAM is widely used in electronic equipment which requires a very low energy consumption, such as portable systems. This advantage applies only to slow SRAMs. The fast SRAM is widely used in cache memory systems (see page 96).

Note   To increase speed and density of integration, the various manufacturers of static RAMs use at least one of the four following approaches:

- A combination of bipolar (TTL or ECL) and CMOS technologies in the design of static RAM chips; this combination produces BiCMOS technology. To counteract the increase in speed, the power dissipated in the chip also increases.
- A reduction in the maximum channel width; this provides a performance increase from the CMOS SRAM fabrication process. With a channel width of 1.5 μm, 64-Kbit SRAMs with access times of 25 ns can be obtained (see Table 4.1).
- The use of GaAs technology to design SRAMs with access times of the order of 1 ns with a capacity of 1 Kbit (Gigabit Logic Inc.).
- Research and development of new RAM architectures which permit increased performance; this approach generally leads to ASMs (see page 85).

Note 1   Some static RAM chips (SRAM) have a battery incorporated to save the data (an example is the Dallas Semiconductor DS1235, a 32K × 8-bit SRAM with an access time of 200 ns which contains a lithium battery permitting the data to be saved in case of failure of the power supplied to the RAM). The lifetime of the battery depends on its composition and the SRAM capacity; some batteries can last for 11 years, such as the MK 48T01/12 SRAM of 1K × 8-bit capacity from Mostek–Thomson Semiconductors.

Note 2   The 'stand-by' mode is initiated when the package is not selected; in this case, the chip select or chip enable pins of the device are not activated.

Note 3   Some devices are described as 'non-volatile random access memories' (NVRAM): examples are the Intel 2001 of 128 × 8 capacity and the 2004 of 512 × 8 capacity. The term non-volatile results from the internal structure which consists of a

Table 4.1 The characteristics of some fast SRAMs.

Type	Manufacturer	Access time (ns)	Capacity	Features
Am99C58	AMD	20	4 K × 4	Power consumption reduced by 70% in stand-by mode.
MCM6288	Motorola	25	16 K × 4	In CMOS technology.
MCM6287	Motorola	25	64 K × 1	In CMOS technology.
HM6787	Hitachi	20	64 K × 1	Dissipates 180 mW in active mode and 34 mW in stand-by. ECL technology.
M5M5256	Mitsubishi	100	32 K × 8	Dissipates 700 mW maximum.
TC55257P	Toshiba	85	32 K × 8	In CMOS technology.
TC518128	Toshiba	120 and 100	1 M bits	This is pseudo-SRAM, an internal refresh circuit is provided on the memory chip.
IDT71256	Integrated	35	32 K × 8	In CMOS technology. The
IDT71257	Device	35	256 K × 1	power dissipated in active
IDT71258	Technology	35	64 K × 4	mode is 300 mW for the 71256 and 400 mW for the 71257 and 71258; in stand-by mode it is 50 μW for the 71256 and 100 μW for the 71257 and 71258.
CAT71C256	Catalyst Semi-conductor	85	32 K × 8	Consumes 5 mW in stand-by mode.
HM6207	Hitachi	25 to 55	256 K × 1	Dissipates 300 mW in active mode and 10 μW in stand-by mode.

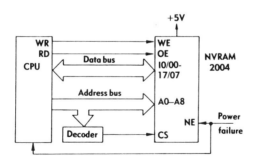

Figure 4.6 Saving data in a non-volatile RAM during a power failure.

static RAM and an EEPROM. The data in the SRAM can be transferred into the EEPROM and vice versa by means of the NE signal (see Fig. 4.6).

When the power supply disappears from the chip, the data contained in the EEPROM section are conserved. The storage duration of information in the EEPROM of the 2001 and 2004 devices is 10 years.

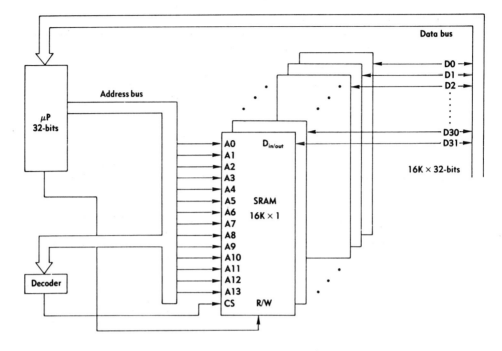

Figure 4.7 Block diagram of a microcomputer with static memory.

Dynamic RAM

Information is stored in the form of a charge in a capacitor which is realized by the gate/substrate capacitance of an MOS transistor. The disadvantage of this type of storage is discharging of the capacitor which leads to the need for periodic refreshing of the information in order to maintain it. This refreshing process is achieved by reading all the data from the DRAM chip and then rewriting the same data into the appropriate addresses. The refresh period varies according to the type of DRAM from 2 to 3 ms.

The advantages of dynamic RAM are:

- Speed.
- Higher integration density (4 Mbit DRAMS are available); this is the most important advantage of DRAMs.

The disadvantages are:

- A high power consumption.
- A higher price than that of slow static RAM since the price of the DRAM is increased by the cost of the necessary additional components (a DRAM controller or refresh circuit).

- The need to provide a refresh circuit (some DRAMs are provided with a refresh system internal to the chip).
- The need to provide DRAM controller circuits (see Fig. 4.8) particularly in the case of DRAMs which use a multiplexed address bus (the RAS pins are 'row address strobe' and CAS are 'column address strobe').

The two multiplexing signals RAS and CAS operate as follows (see Fig. 4.9). The RAS signal is active first and this indicates that the address bits correspond to row decoding; the CAS signal then becomes active, which indicates selection, across the address bits, of a column from the row selected previously by the RAS signal. This multiplexed mode provides an economy of pins equivalent to the chip address bus width.

Application specific memory (ASM)

In most cases, these are read/write memory devices, either static or dynamic, which are dedicated to specific applications. They are chips which combine memory with one or more other functions. ASMs are of two types:

Semi-custom ASMs. These are devices which include the support logic required for direct connection to the system bus on the chip; this saves space and reduces costs. One ASM chip, in some cases, can replace up to 100 low integration density chips. Some chips contain predefined networks in addition to the RAM; these are 'gate array memories'.

Full-custom ASMs. These are RAMs designed specifically on request for a defined application. New functions are added to the storage provided by the RAM; in some cases this can affect the architecture of the memory itself. Examples are:

(a) The addition of an arithmetic and logic unit (ALU) to the chip; this permits manipulation and organization of data independently of the microprocessor. This type of chip is called a 'smart memory'.
(b) The addition of data testing circuits within the chip.
(c) The facility to modify the RAM organization (for example, the Hitachi HD 63310 can be configured as 1 K × 8 bits or as two FIFO shift registers).

Other types of ASM are available, such as:

- 'Cache-tag' RAMs which are dedicated to multiprocessor applications (see page 96).
- Video RAMs which are dedicated to image acquisition applications (see Fig. 4.33).
- Double port, or dual access, RAMs which are dedicated to bit-slice micro-processor-based applications, fast graphic systems and dual microprocessor systems. In the last case, the dual access RAM can be used as a communication system between two microprocessors for passing information while ensuring independent operation of each microprocessor (see Fig. 4.10).

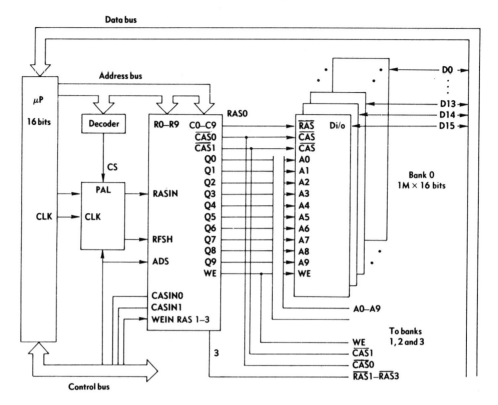

Figure 4.8 Block diagram of a 4M × 16-bit dynamic memory with a DRAM controller. The role of the DRAM controller is to handle the control signals, to refresh the DRAMs while arbitrating between memory refresh and access cycles, and to control the multiplexed DRAM bus (by rows 'RAS' and columns 'CAS').

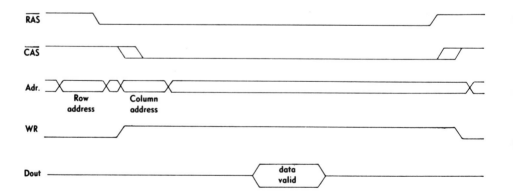

Figure 4.9 DRAM read cycle with a multiplexed address bus (the RAS and CAS signals must be present).

Table 4.2 The characteristics of some DRAMs.

Type	Manufacturer	Access time (ns)	Capacity	Features
51C258L	Intel	120 to 200	64 K × 4	Power dissipated: 250 mW (active mode), 500 μW (stand-by).
KM41256	Samsung semi-conductor	100 to 150	256 K × 4	Power dissipated: 1 W. Available from several other RAM manufacturers.
MT1512	Micron technology	120 to 200	512 K × 1	Power dissipated: 300 mW (active mode), 120 mW (stand-by).
MT9064	Micron technology	120 to 200	64 K × 1	Power dissipated: 675 mW (active mode), 135 mW (stand-by).
IMS2800	Inmos	60	256 K × 1	CMOS technology.
TC511000P	Toshiba	85	1 M × 1	CMOS technology.
TC514100J	Toshiba	150	4 M × 1	CMOS technology. Power dissipated: 330 mW (active mode) 5.5 mW (stand-by).

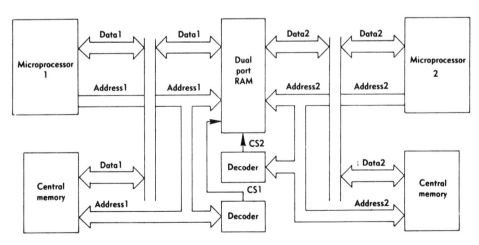

Figure 4.10 Two microprocessors sharing a RAM by the use of a double port RAM. The latter can be considered as a 'letter box' in the process of passing information between the two microprocessors.

The advantages of ASMs are as follows:

- A saving of printed circuit board space.
- A saving in cost for complex examples.
- A reduction in development time.
- The capability of reconfiguring the RAM organization.
- The possibility of making a number of functions available in addition to that of storing information (examples are counters and information processing within the ASM independently of the microprocessor).
- An increase in performance due to elimination of signal propagation delays in inter-chip connections.

4.7.2 Read Only Memory (ROM)

Programs and fixed data can reside in a permanent manner, without the need for modification, in non-volatile or read only memory. The contents of this type of memory cannot be modified, it is programmed once and for all. In particular, ROMs are programmed by mask during fabrication of the chip and PROMs are programmed by the user by accessing memory cells containing fusible links. Several types of read only memory are available to the user according to the state of advancement of the product – ROMs, PROMs, EPROMs etc.

Read only memory (ROM) chips are for reading only, since the data have been written once and for all during the design of the chip; the data are communicated to the chip manufacturer by the designer of the code.

Programmable read only memory (PROM) devices can be programmed by the code designer with the help of a PROM/EPROM programming unit. They cannot be erased and reprogrammed and do not permit error correction; the quantity consumed would be very high in the design phase. ROMs and PROMs are used only for production of the product.

The other type of currently used read only memory is EPROM; EPROMs are ROMs which can be erased by ultraviolet light using an 'EPROM eraser', which exposes them to ultraviolet light at 2500 Å for 20 minutes, and reprogrammed with an EPROM programmer (see Chapter 5). EPROMs are used in the prototype development phases.

In addition to ROMs, PROMs and EPROMs, other types of read only memory are used such as programmable logic arrays (PLA), programmable array logic (PAL), erasable programmable logic devices (EPLD), electrically erasable programmable logic devices (EEPLD) (see Chapter 2) and electrically erasable programmable read only memories (EEPROM). The last are memories which can be erased and reprogrammed electrically (based on the Fowler–Nordheim tunnel effect).

In certain cases, EEPROMs can be used as RAMs which will be erased, not after a power failure as is the case with RAMs, but voluntarily by the operator of a product which contains an internal EEPROM erasure and programming circuit. The

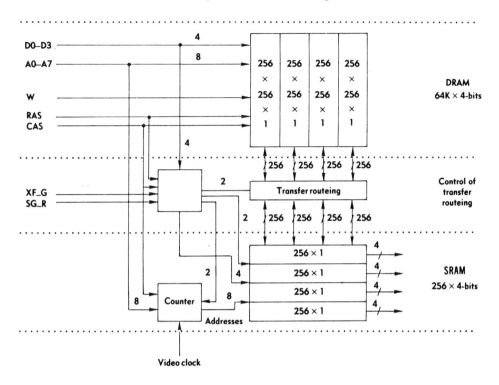

Figure 4.11 Internal structure of the Am90C644 chip. Using CMOS technology, two types of RAM coexist on the chip – static RAM with a capacity of 256 × 4 bits operating in the form of a shift register and DRAM with a capacity of 64K × 4 bits (buffer memory). The two RAMs can exchange data using an internal on-chip transfer bus; an internal transfer of 1024 bits (256 × 4) can be made in less than 200 ns. When the internal transfer is not active, the two RAMs can be used separately. The DRAM part of the chip could, for example, be updated by the CPU or an image-acquisition system such as a camera. During this time the SRAM part could send information to the display in the form of serial data.

programming voltage to be applied varies according to the EEPROM from 24 V to 18 V; some EEPROMs can be programmed with voltages of 12 V (the 48128 EEPROM from Seeq Technology) or even 3 V (the MSM28C64A from Catalyst Semiconductor) (see Table 4.4).

4.7.3 Memory Management Units

The power of 16- and 32-bit microprocessors permits the design of multitasking and multi-user products (comparable with the facilities found on minicomputers); as with minicomputers, the microprocessor requires a memory management system.

Table 4.3 The characteristics of some application-specific memories (ASM).

Type	Manufacturer	Access time (ns)	Capacity	Features
2001	Intel	180 to 300	128 × 8	NVRAM. The internal structure consists of an SRAM and an EEPROM.
Am9151	AMD	40	1 K × 4	SRAM. Error detection facility available on the chip.
CY7C132	Cypress Semi-conductor	35	2 K × 8	SRAM. Dual port RAM.
Am90C644	AMD		256 × 4 and 64 K × 4	Two types of RAM are available on the chip: 256 × 4 of SRAM (shift register) and 64 K × 4 of DRAM (buffer) (see Fig. 4.11).
ET2009M	Fujitsu	5 RAM access	4 × 256 × 9	In ECL and TTL technology; the chip contains 9 Kbits of RAM and a gate array of 1920 gates.
AAA3081K	NMB Semi-conductor	13 to 20	256 K × 16	Video RAM with a serial port.
AAA3082K	NMB Semi-conductor	25 to 40	256 K × 8 × 2	Dual port video RAM.
BT450	Brooktree Corporation	30 MHZ and 50 MHZ		Video RAM containing: 16 × 12 dual port RAM for the colour palette, 3 × 12 dual port RAM for the palette overlay, three 4-bit DACs for the three colour video outputs (RGB). Power consumption is 920mW (maximum).

The memory management system associated with the central processing unit (the microprocessor) must resolve the following problems which can arise in a multitasking or multi-user system:

- Use of the same memory area by several programs (multitasking or multi-user).
- Translation of addresses during program loading.
- Organization and storage of memory-resident programs and data.
- Generation of an interrupt or error message in the case of access to a non-existent memory area.
- Increase of available memory space (use of virtual memory).

To control the memory, the microprocessor makes use of a memory management circuit (this can be directly integrated into the microprocessor chip, as in the case of

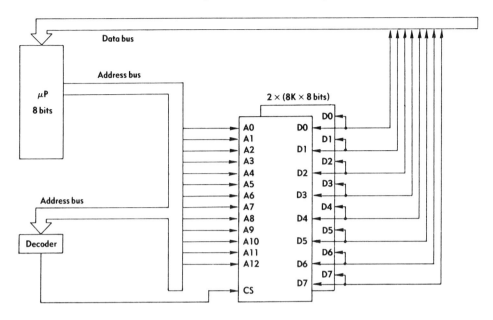

Figure 4.12 Block diagram of a read only memory consisting of two EPROM chips, each of 8K × 8 bits.

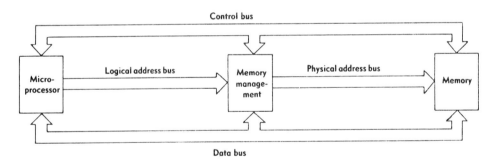

Figure 4.13 Block diagram of the connections between a memory management unit and the microprocessor.

the Motorola MC 68030 microprocessor). The main function of this chip, the memory management unit (MMU), is to assign a program to memory in accordance with the translation rules (see Fig. 4.13).

Two types of approach are used by the various manufacturers; these are page addressing (examples are the Zilog Z8015, the Motorola MC68851 and the National Semiconductor NS16082) and segmented addressing (examples are the Motorola

Table 4.4   The characteristics of some EPROMS and EEPROMS.

Type	Manufacturer	Access time (ns)	Capacity	Features
27916	Intel	250	16 K × 8	EEPROM, similar to the 27128 EPROM but has a random number generator and encrypting logic on the chip. Used in systems for protection against unauthorized access.
2716	Intel	450 to 650	2 K × 8	EPROM.
38C32	Seeq Technology	35	4 K × 8	EEPROM. Dissipates 350 mW in active mode and has the circuits required for reprogramming on the chip. The circuit requires a supply of 5 V.
2764	Intel	200 to 450	8 K × 8	EPROM.
27128	Intel	150	16 K × 8	EPROM.
WS57C256F	WaferScale Integration	55	32 K × 8	EPROM. Dissipates 300 mW at 10 MHz.
AT28C256	Atmel	150 to 350	32 K × 8	EEPROM. Dissipates 440 mW in active mode and 550 μW in stand-by mode.
27512	Intel	200	64 K × 8	EPROM.
Am27C1024	AMD	200	64 K × 16	EPROM.
CY7C261	Cypress Semi-conductor	35 to 55	8 K × 8	EPROM. Dissipates 500 mW in active mode and 100 mW in stand-by mode.
WS57C257	WaferScale Integration	50 to 55	16 K × 16	EPROM. Dissipates 325 mW in active mode and 75 mW in stand-by mode.
MSM28C64A	Catalyst and OKI Semi-conduct-or	120	16 K × 4	EEPROM operates with a supply of 3 V for a dissipation of 49.5 mW in active mode and 22.5 mW in stand-by mode at a frequency of 8 MHz. Erasure of the EEPROM is achieved internally by changing the supply from 3 V to 18 V.
μPD27 C1024 D	NEC	150/200 and 250	64 K × 16	EPROM. Dissipates 50 mA (max.) in active mode and 100 μA (max.) in stand-by mode.
TC571000	Toshiba	200	128 K × 8	EPROM.

MC68451 and the Zilog Z8010). These two approaches can also be combined (examples are the Signetics/Philips 68905 and the Zilog Z8015).

In general, in the case of page addressing the memory is divided into a number of pages of constant length (the actual length is associated with the type of MMU circuit used), while in segmented mode the page length is variable.

Each memory segment or page is associated with a descriptor which is one register of a table containing information which relates the physical address and the state of protection of the page or segment.

The following sections give the principles of these two addressing modes. The developer should examine the details and special features of the MMU in the context of the choices made for the product; the techniques suggested vary according to the component manufacturer.

Page addressing

The logical address is divided into two parts (see Fig. 4.14):

- *The segment number.* The memory management unit (MMU) uses this part as an address to a segment table; the contents of this table give the page address and form the most significant part of the physical address.
- *The page index.* This defines the place in the page.

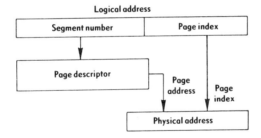

Figure 4.14 Translation of a logical address into a physical address (page addressing).

Segmented addressing

The logical address is divided into two parts (see Fig. 4.15):

- *The offset.* The offset or displacement of the segment.
- *The segment number.* This number is used to address a table of descriptors. This table contains the start address of the segment (the Base Address in physical memory) and this address is added to the offset of the segment.

Comment Some systems, such as the Zilog Z8010, divide the displacement field into two parts, the more significant part being added to the segment start address and the less significant part forming the displacement (see Fig. 4.16).

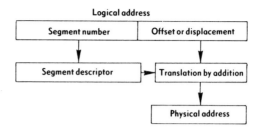

Figure 4.15 Translation of a logical address into a physical address (segmented addressing).

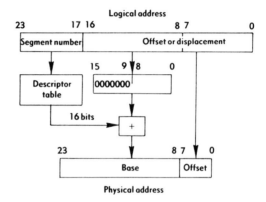

Figure 4.16 Memory management mechanism of the Zilog Z8010.

Memory management of the Z8010 corresponds to the memory management mechanisms used in the PDP11/34 minicomputer; the only difference is that the displacement field (or offset) is of 13 bits for the PDP11/34 and of 17 bits for the Z8010.

Note Other functions associated with memory management and previously reserved for large systems, such as protection for particular memory areas (e.g. that reserved for the operating system) against unauthorized access, are available on several 32-bit microprocessors (for example the Intel 80386).

4.7.4 Address Decoding

The purpose of address decoding is to permit selection of different electronic packages in accordance with the addresses defined in the memory map (see Fig. 2.11). Switching between ROM/RAM and other programmable packages, such as

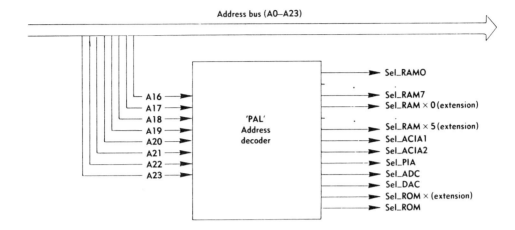

Figure 4.17   Address decoding. A programmable array logic (PAL) device is used
to generate the various selection signals.

data converters, peripheral interfaces etc., is achieved by means of the address
decoder (see Fig. 4.17).

4.8   Direct Memory Access (DMA)

Direct memory access (DMA) is used when it is necessary to transfer a large volume
of data from the memory to a peripheral (see Fig. 4.18) or another memory such as
the RAM of another microprocessor or mass memory. This process requires a high
execution speed and consequently it is achieved without using CPU control
instructions. Several types of DMA can be used such as halting the microprocessor,
cycle stealing and multiplexing.

The most commonly used DMA system operates in the microprocessor halt mode;
it is executed in the following sequence:

- A peripheral makes a DMA request.
- The CPU terminates the instruction in progress.
- The CPU recognizes the DMA request.
- The data and address buses are freed by the CPU.
- The peripheral uses the bus to transfer the data to or from memory.
- The peripheral returns control to the CPU at the end of the transfer.
- The CPU regains control of the bus and continues executing instructions.

DMA in microprocessor halt mode is the fastest mode of transfer; its speed is
determined by the cycle time of the memory. For example, with a memory cycle time
of 200 ns, the transfer can be made at a frequency of 5 MHz. This speed must,

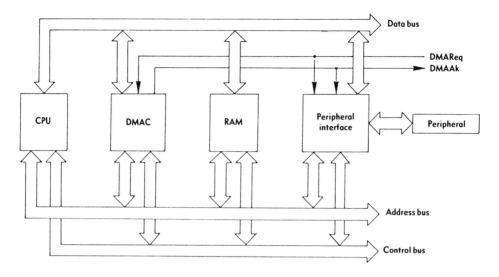

Figure 4.18 Block diagram of a system containing a DMA controller.

however, take account of any possible limitations in the transfer time of the peripheral which is receiving or transmitting the data by DMA. When this situation arises, it is preferable to use one of the two other modes of DMA (cycle stealing and multiplexing) or to connect the peripheral to a high-capacity buffer.

To execute DMA, it is necessary to use a DMA control chip (see Fig. 4.18); each microprocessor manufacturer markets a DMA controller to support its microprocessor.

4.9 Cache Memory

In the design of microprocessor-based products which require high speeds (such as 32-bit devices or bit-slice microprocessors), memory accesses must be equally fast. Three techniques for the design of read/write memory are suggested as follows:

- The use of DRAMs with access times from 100 to 120 ns; this requires the introduction of a 'wait state' to allow for the relative slowness of the memory with respect to the capabilities of the microprocessor (particularly in the case of 32-bit microprocessors) and involves slowing down the CPU.
- The use of fast SRAMs of 50–60 ns; this increases the cost of the product and the power dissipated requires a large printed circuit area (see page 82).
- The use of cache memory (see Fig. 4.19).

A cache memory is a very fast memory of relatively small storage capacity which is located between the microprocessor and central memory (see Fig. 4.19). It is

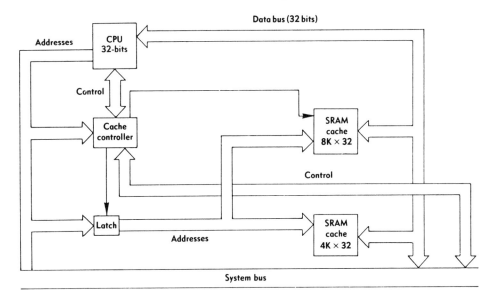

Figure 4.19 Block diagram of a system containing a cache memory.

generally in the form of a data buffer or 'data cache' and an address buffer or 'cache tag'. The information contained in central memory which is most frequently requested by the CPU should preferably be stored in the cache memory. Operation occurs in the following sequence:

- The microprocessor makes a data request to the central memory.
- The cache controller checks whether the address sent by the CPU corresponds to a cache-tag address.
- If it corresponds, the corresponding data at the cache-tag address, which is contained in the data buffer of the cache memory, is sent to the CPU.
- If it does not correspond, the CPU accesses the central memory directly.

Loading of cache memory is achieved in various ways which depend on the type of microprocessor, the availability of an MMU (see page 89) and the specification of the product to be realized. A cache controller is also necessary (examples are the 82385 from Austek Microsystems Ltd and the μPD 43608R from NEC Electronic Inc.).

Cache memory systems can be either of two types:

- *Direct-mapped.* The address sent by the microprocessor is compared with the addresses contained in a 'tag memory' or 'cache tag'; if the two addresses are identical, then the corresponding data are contained in the cache memory. In this mode, there is a memory location for each address. This is the least costly form of cache memory system.

- *Associative mode*. Associative cache memory does not involve searching for data whose storage address is known. The search is for information which is contained in memory and is called a 'descriptor' or 'key' and has information associated with it. This technique corresponds to addressing by content. In this mode, two or four locations in cache memory are used for each memory address.

Note 1   To avoid wait states, the access time of the memory must be less than $2/F$, where F is the microprocessor clock frequency. If the memory cannot achieve this speed, a change to a configuration using cache memory is recommended.

Note 2   To improve the performance of the product, cache memory can also be used for interfaces with peripheral systems such as high-resolution interactive graphic systems and high-capacity mass memories such as a hard disk.

4.10   The Clock

The clock defines the operating rate of the microcomputer, both the microprocessor itself and other devices which require clock signals (see Fig. 4.20). The majority of microprocessors make use of an independent clock circuit but some have a clock circuit incorporated on the microprocessor chip itself.

4.11   Systems with Coprocessors

The coprocessor is most often a mathematical processor having its own instructions; this instruction set controls the mathematical operations (examples of mathematical coprocessors are 8087, 80187, 80287, 80387, MC68881, Am9511 etc.).
   Devices of this type are particularly desirable when anticipated programs contain a large number of mathematical calculations. Incorporating this type of processor (see Fig. 4.21) relieves the microprocessor of the long times required for certain mathematical operations in fixed and floating point, such as arithmetic operations, trigonometric functions and the testing of these programs. The availability of this chip considerably improves product performance and reduces the development and testing time of the software associated with mathematical processing.

4.12   Multiprocessor Systems

A multiprocessor system is the solution to problems such as the following which cannot be resolved with a single processor.

- Excessively slow routeing of data.
- A need for higher performance.

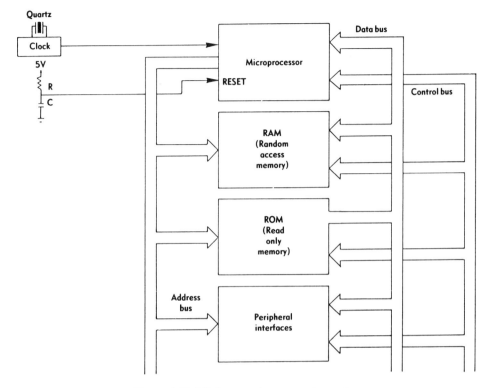

Figure 4.20 Minimum microcomputer system.

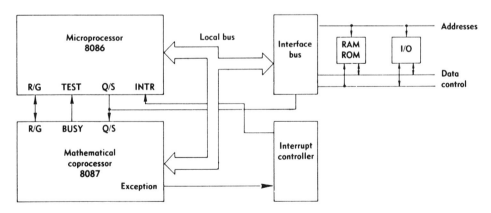

Figure 4.21 Block diagram of the connections between a microprocessor and a coprocessor. The TEST and BUSY signals ensure synchronization between the two processors. The request/grant signal (R/G) provides arbitration in the use of the local bus which is common to the two processors. The EXCEPTION and INTR signals indicate the occurrence of exceptional events such as errors. The Q/S signal (queue status and S-lines) indicates to the 8087 the presence of instructions on the bus and the initiation of input/outputs.

- An excessive rate of occupation of the microprocessor.
- Excessively slow response time.
- The need to provide a product which can execute two or more processes simultaneously.
- The need to provide a multi-user system with support for a large number of simultaneous users.
- The need to run several operating systems simultaneously.
- The need to provide a system for recovering control of the system in the case where one microprocessor becomes inoperative (i.e. fault tolerant systems).

According to the requirements and specification of the product, various types of architecture are suggested. The choice is influenced by the following:

- Processing speeds.
- The similarity, or otherwise, of the microprocessors installed in the product.
- The memory capacities required for each microprocessor and the shared memory capacity.
- The memory access times.

There are essentially three types of multiprocessor system, as discussed in Sections 4.12.1–3.

4.12.1 Multiprocessor Systems with Shared Common Memory

A common memory is assigned to the whole set of microprocessors (see Fig. 4.22); each microprocessor accesses this memory through a bus system which is common to all the microprocessors. The main disadvantage of this type of configuration is the low speed, which can cause bottlenecks if several memory access requests occur at the same time.

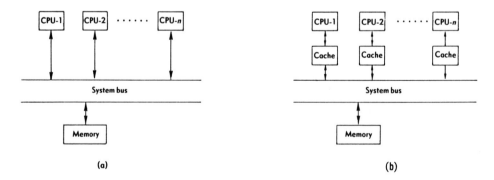

Figure 4.22 Multiprocessor system with shared common memory: (a) without cache memory; (b) with cache memory.

4.12.2 Multiprocessor Systems with Shared Local Memory

Each microprocessor can use a local memory while retaining the facility of accessing the local memory of other processors by way of a common bus system (see Fig. 4.23).

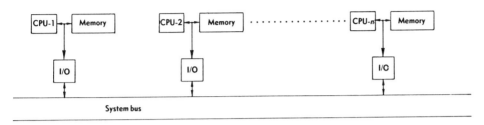

Figure 4.23 Multiprocessor system with shared local memory.

4.12.3 Multiprocessor Systems with a Communication Protocol

Each microprocessor can use a local memory and also access the local memory of other processors by observing a protocol during use of the communication bus (see Fig. 4.24). With this type of configuration, it is not necessary to use microprocessors of the same type or from the same manufacturer.

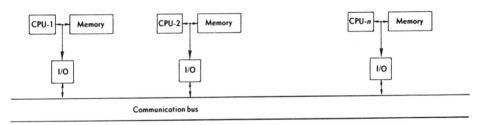

Figure 4.24 Microprocessors in a network

4.13 Interrupts

When any peripheral (telephone, keyboard, hard or floppy disk, alarm detector etc.) or other internal system element (watchdog, coprocessor etc.) wishes to signal an event to the microprocessor, the microprocessor can act on this request by one of two methods:

- Periodic examination of the status registers of the various peripheral interface devices. This method can waste a large amount of processor time due to testing the flags in different status registers in addition to the delay in providing the service.
- An interrupt signal.

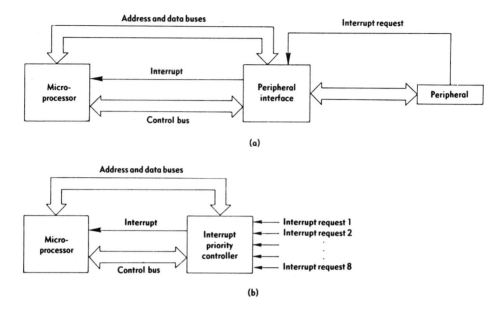

Figure 4.25 (a) Block diagram of interrupt generation by a peripheral; (b) block diagram of the connection of an interrupt priority controller to a basic microprocessor system.

Operation by interrupt is instantaneous; as soon as the interrupt signal is activated, the microprocessor terminates the instruction which is being executed, saves the context and services the interrupt by executing the program associated with the interrupt. If several devices need to make an interrupt request, selection organized by priority can be provided using a device called a priority interrupt controller, see Fig. 4.25.

4.14 Peripherals

Peripherals are those devices which are directly accessible to humans (see Figs 4.26 and 4.27), either for input of information (for processing and storage by the microcomputer) or output of information such as the results of processing provided by the microcomputer.

Standard peripherals are a keyboard, a screen, a printer, a floppy disk drive and a hard disk drive. Additional equipment includes a modem (for telephone communication), transducers (temperature, pressure, humidity, threshold detectors etc.), industrial machines (e.g. motors), plotting tables, mice etc.

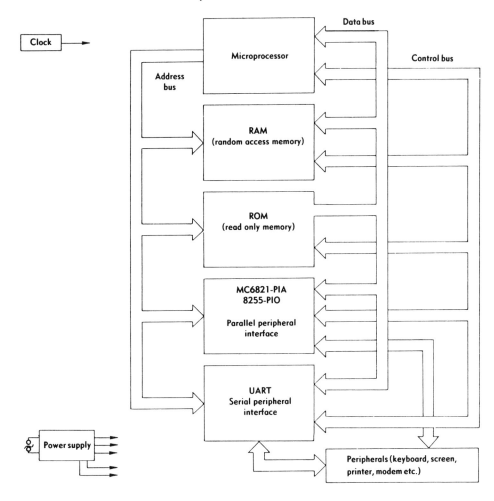

Figure 4.26 Complete microcomputer system with peripherals.

4.15 Peripheral Interface Devices

The peripheral interface device, more briefly called the 'interface', is the device which permits communication between two different worlds. It is the area where information is passed between the world of man, or at least his intermediary in the form of a peripheral, and that of the microprocessor (see Fig. 4.27). The timescale changes from the second or millisecond to the microsecond.

The most common peripherals (printer, keyboard, telephone line etc.) make use of serial or parallel interfaces and, without exception, are not connected directly to the microprocessor bus (see also page 115).

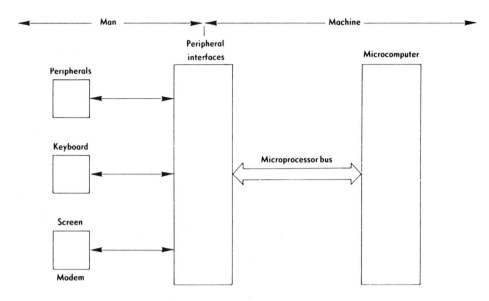

Figure 4.27 Communication between two worlds (man and machine).

In the subsequent part of this section, several examples of interconnection to peripherals commonly encountered in a microprocessor-based product will be presented.

4.15.1   Parallel Interfaces

Almost all microprocessor manufacturers provide parallel interface devices. Examples are the Motorola MC 6821, the Intel 8255, the Zilog Z8420 and so on. A parallel interface permits higher-speed links than serial ones; this makes them preferable for some types of equipment such as:

- Electronic power control (see Fig. 4.30).
- Digital-to-analogue and analogue-to-digital converters (see Figs 4.44 and 4.45).
- Fast printers.
- Instrumentation (e.g. IEEE-488).
- Keyboards etc.

When a parallel interface device is not available from the microprocessor manufacturer, an equivalent circuit can be realized by using three-state buffers and a number of logic devices for control (see Fig. 4.28).

All the signals handled by parallel interface devices can be programmed independently either as inputs or as outputs (see Fig. 4.29). The power electronic

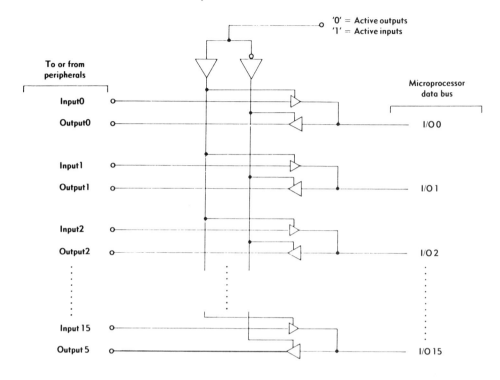

Figure 4.28 The use of three-state buffers as a parallel interface.

interface controls high-power devices. To operate these devices correctly, it is necessary to protect the interface interconnections (the digital signals) from the high-power signals with isolating circuits such as optocouplers (see Fig. 4.30).

4.15.2 Serial Interfaces

Various types of serial interface device are available, both synchronous and asynchronous, which permit microprocessor systems to communicate with each other or with peripherals which require a serial link such as modems, printers and so on. Serial interface devices are connected to the system bus. The majority of peripherals which operate in serial mode use an RS-232 link (see Fig. 4.31).

4.15.3 Display Interfaces

Every product requires to display information for the operator. In this section, the most commonly used types of interface are described.

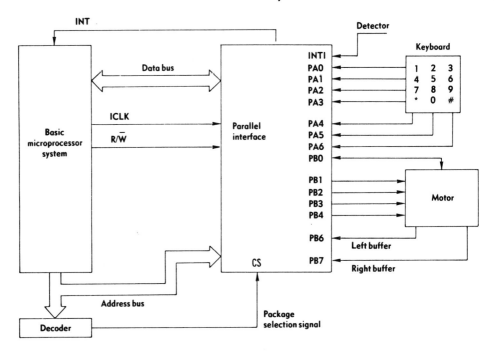

Figure 4.29 Programmable parallel interface device. Signals PA0–PA7 and PB0–PB7 can be programmed independently as inputs or outputs in accordance with the requirements of the product to be realized.

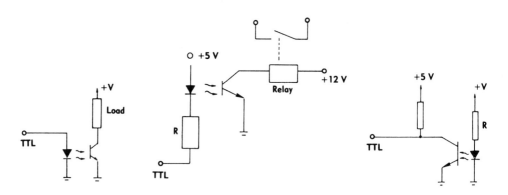

Figure 4.30 Power interface circuits.

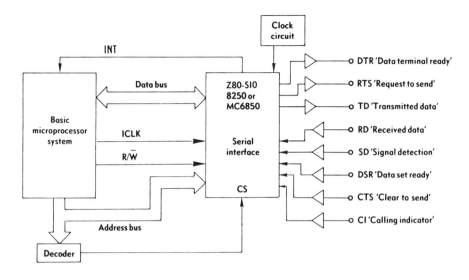

Figure 4.31 Block diagram of an RS232 link.

ROM character generation

Until the introduction of high-resolution screens and displays based on other types of technology (such as plasma and LCD) the majority of character and graphic display systems were based on the display of distinct symbols using character and graphic patterns stored in ROM (see Fig. 4.32).

The major disadvantage of this type of interface is the difficulty of changing the characters without hardware modification (i.e. changing the character ROM).

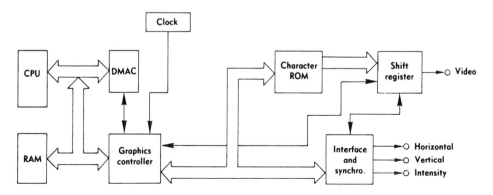

Figure 4.32 A system for displaying characters stored in ROM.

Bit-mapped characters and graphics

All characters and symbols are defined in a software 'font' file; this file is loaded into memory each time power is applied. The main advantage of this approach is that the form of the characters and other symbols can be modified entirely by software (see page 44). Since the start of the 1980s the 'bit-map' concept has taken the place of the character generating ROM.

In a bit-mapped display, each point of the screen is associated with one or more bits in memory which give information on the state of the point, whether it is light or dark, its colour and its display mode (such as inverse video or blinking). The microprocessor can use this information to perform various graphical operations on the point.

To provide a system with a bit-mapped display, the product must have a 16- or 32-bit microprocessor and a large 'video' memory capacity which holds an image of the whole screen. This capacity is related to the resolution; for example, a screen of 1024 × 1024 pixels requires a minimum memory of 128K bytes and addressing space for 1 048 576 pixels.

Note In products with a bit-mapped display, functions associated with graphic creation and manipulation (such as windows and special patterns) are generally available in the operating system for use in application software.

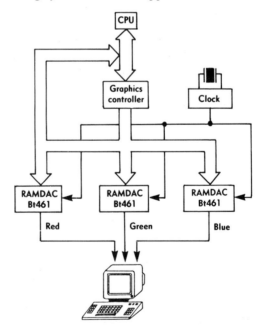

Figure 4.33 Block diagram of a colour display interface. The characters are in bit-map form in a software file. The latter is loaded by the operating system on each application of power or by a utility.

Digital display interfaces

Various other types of display have appeared on the market such as plasma, LCD, electromechanical, electrophoretic, electroluminescent and so on. The majority of new displays are digital rather than analogue; this provides vast opportunities for entirely digital products such as television and digital telephones with an LCD display.

LCD displays cost less and consume very little energy in comparison with other types such as plasma and electroluminescent types; this makes them particularly attractive for portable products.

In spite of their newness and the development of LCD devices (such as improvements in colour, polarization resistance at low and high temperatures, contrast, viewing angle, response time etc.) displays using LCD technology are more and more widely used particularly in portable computers, printers, multimeters, pocket colour televisions and car dashboard televisions (for example in the Ford Thunderbird).

The molecules of liquid crystals change the nature of the transmitted light when voltages are applied (see Fig. 4.34) as a consequence of modification to the orientation of the molecules.

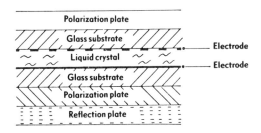

Figure 4.34 The component parts of an LCD display.

The structure of an LCD display is as follows (see Fig. 4.34): two glass substrates which retain the liquid crystal, transparent vertical and horizontal electrodes which form a matrix located within these two substrates (in contact with the liquid crystal), two polarization plates for the two electrodes and a reflection plate.

LCD displays interface with the microprocessor by means of an LCD display controller (see Figs 4.35 and 4.36). These controllers ensure reception of the data sent by the microprocessor for display, transmission of these data to the LCD display and the cursor control functions.

The main types of LCD are listed in Table 4.5; other technologies are in the course of development, particularly the active matrix.

Note The various technologies listed in Table 4.5 are based on modifications to the molecular composition of liquid crystals which influence the orientation of molecules

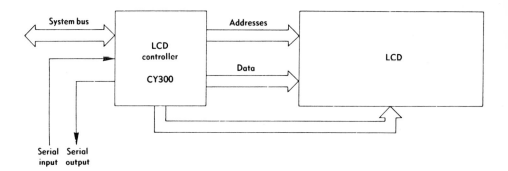

Figure 4.35 Block diagram of LCD display control in parallel or serial mode.

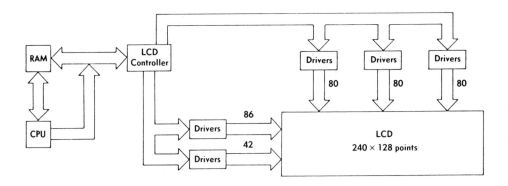

Figure 4.36 Block diagram of interfacing with an LCD display. In the design of an LCD display, drivers are necessary for each point on the display.

Table 4.5 Comparison of some technologies used in LCDs.

Technology	Contrast	Viewing angle	Response time
TN 'twisted nematic'	<4	<30°	150 ms
STN 'super twisted nematic'	7–8	60°	180 ms
SBE 'super twisted birefringence effect'	8	60°	350–500 ms
Ferroelectric	10	60°	80 ms
TFT 'thin film transistor'	10	60°	80 ms
MIM 'metal–insulator–metal'	10	60°	100 ms

when voltages are applied to the two electrodes. All of these phenomena affect the light emitted by the LCD.

LCD technology is recent and has some disadvantages; the following are being improved:

- *Limited contrast.* The ratio between illuminated and dark points on an LCD display using super twisted nematic (STN) materials is of the order of 7. For satisfactory readability this ratio must be greater than 2.
- *Visibility limitation with angle of view.* In STN technology this angle can reach 60° (see Fig. 4.37).
- *Limitations in the operating temperature range caused by polarization.* This range which was from 0°C to 50°C has been improved to −30°C to 80°C.
- *Response time.* This varies from 80 ms to 150 ms according to the technology.

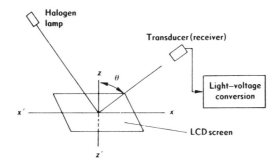

Figure 4.37 Measuring the viewing angle of an LCD display.

To reduce the disadvantages of small viewing angle and inadequate contrast, backlighting is used. The major disadvantage of this is the large volume occupied and the increased overall weight.

In some products having a large area LCD display, several light sources are used; precautions must then be taken to make the junctions between areas illuminated by different light sources invisible and to distribute the light homogeneously over the whole surface of the screen.

4.15.4 Floppy and Hard Disk Interface Units

Two types of mass memory are found in microprocessor-based products; these are floppy disk units and hard disk units.

The proliferation of floppy and hard disk units encourages the definition of a standard interface between the microprocessor bus and peripheral mass memories. This requires as many manufacturers as possible to adhere to a number of standards;

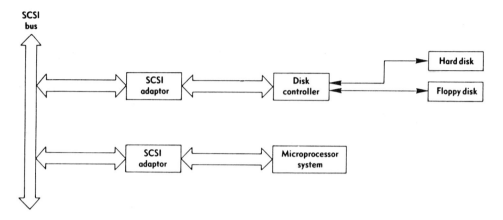

Figure 4.38 Block diagram of connections with the SCSI bus.

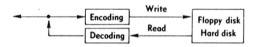

Figure 4.39 Information decoding and encoding.

the 'small computer systems interface' (SCSI) has been defined with this aim (see Fig. 4.38). Use of the SCSI interface is not limited to floppy and hard disk peripheral units; other peripherals can be connected to this type of bus.

Recordings on floppy and hard disks pass through a system of encoding and decoding during writing and reading (see Fig. 4.39); this process occurs in a disk controller circuit.

The following are among the most frequently used recording modes:

- *Non-return to zero (NRZ)*. In this recording mode, the only reference states are saturation magnetization of the magnetic layer in opposite directions; there is no return to a neutral magnetic state after recording a 1 or a 0.
- *Frequency modulation (FM)*. The data bits are transformed so that a bit of value 1 involves a change of flux and a bit of value 0 does not. Clock signals are located at the start of each binary element and this permits perfect synchronization.
- *Modified frequency modulation* (MFM). This is identical to the FM mode except that flux changes are recorded at three distinct frequencies (F, $2F$ and $\frac{1}{2}F$) according to the data sequence. This mode is used particularly in 5¼-inch hard disks.
- *2,7 run length limited (RLL)*. Very similar to the MFM mode, the 2,7 RLL mode is used on large systems (the IBM 3370 family from 1979). As a result of the availability of large storage capacities, the 2,7 RLL mode is used increasingly in

microcomputers. In 2,7 RLL recordings, the number of zeros between ones is defined; the data have at least 2 and at most 7 zeros separated by ones, hence the numbers 2,7.

Floppy disk interface unit

A floppy disk is a mass memory of small dimensions in the form of a flexible disk covered on both faces with a magnetic material on which the data is recorded. A floppy disk is organized in tracks and sectors; input/output is in serial form and the most frequently used encoding is frequency modulation (FM). The removable floppy disk is placed in the drive unit before use.

The disk drive unit includes a mechanical section containing a stepper motor which permits displacement of the read/write head and a power electronic interface (motor and relay control). Control of the floppy disk unit by the system is achieved by means of the following signals (see Fig. 4.40):

- *Write:* serial information is written onto the disk in accordance with the type of encoding chosen.
- *Read:* serial information is read from the disk.
- *Sel-unit:* this enables selection of one unit from several when the disk controller can control several disk units.
- *Write-protect:* a signal which indicates that the floppy disk is protected against writing. This signal is activated if a tab is put on the notch of a floppy disk.
- *Direction:* indicates the direction of displacement of the read/write head.
- *Step:* a signal which contains pulses corresponding to the number of steps of displacement of the read/write head; the direction is indicated by the 'direction' signal.

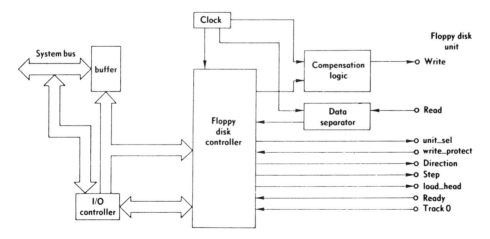

Figure 4.40 Block diagram of the connections to a floppy disk controller.

- *Load-head:* activates the read/write head to perform a read or write operation.
- *Ready:* indicates that the floppy disk is correctly located, it has achieved the correct speed of rotation and is ready for input and output operations.
- *Track 0:* indicates that the read/write head is located on track 0.

Although the specific details relating to each floppy disk controller vary, the following, which form the interface with the disk drive unit, are available on most floppy disk controllers (see Fig. 4.40):

- The buffer which amplifies the various signals.
- The input/output controller.
- The circuits which generate the interface signals with a DMA controller; these permit data transfer from central memory to the floppy disk and vice versa.
- The status register or registers which handle the various disk drive status signals (for example, an indication of the presence of the floppy disk in the disk drive unit).
- A circuit for the interrupt signal generated by the disk controller; this signal permits the microprocessor to read the status register mentioned above and to determine the actions to be taken according to the contents of this register.
- The clock circuit which provides the clock signals for the various interface functions, particularly encoding and decoding the recordings.
- The data separator. The data read from the disk contain both clock signals and data, the data separator enables the data and clock signals to be recovered from the recording contained on the disk.
- The control register enables the different functions to be initialized, such as the type of disk ($3\frac{1}{2}$, $5\frac{1}{4}$ or 8 inches), RESET (reset to zero of all the disk interface registers), read or write control, halt transfer between central memory and the disk.
- The compensation block. During a write operation, problems associated with the magnetic configuration can influence correct positioning of the head. The compensation block enables these problems to be overcome by the introduction of a correcting delay during reading of a recording.
- A shift register which converts parallel data into serial data.
- A data register or buffer register which contains the data during read and write operations.
- A sector register which contains the address of the required sector.
- A track register which contains the number of the track on which the head is positioned.

Hard disk interface

In a hard disk unit, the floppy disk is replaced by a set of disks in the form of a superposed stack (see Fig. 4.41) which has a read/write head for each of the two faces of each disk. The head-supporting arms are interdependent. Those tracks which face the heads in one position of the arms constitute a cylinder.

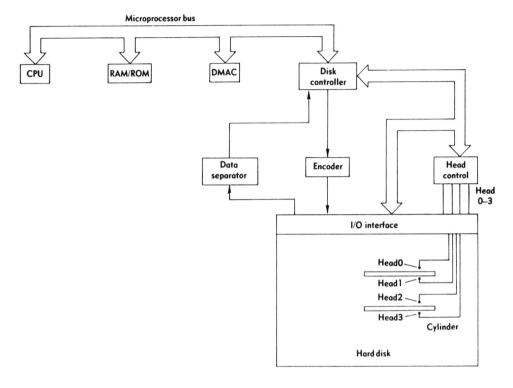

Figure 4.41 Block diagram of the connections to a hard disk controller.

The descriptions given previously in the section on floppy disk interface units remain valid for interfacing with a hard disk; access to a sector of the hard disk merely requires the head number and cylinder number in addition to the sector number.

Note   A number of floppy disk controllers can also support hard disks; an example is the Signetics SCN 68454-IMDC (intelligent multiple disk controller).

4.15.5   Analogue-to-Digital and Digital-to-Analogue Converters

Analogue-to-digital converters are used to acquire information which is in analogue form (see page 118). Digital-to-analogue converters are required to drive peripherals which operate with analogue signals such as a cathode ray tube display.
   The choice of converter is based on:

● The resolution – the number of data bits in the digital section of the converter.
● The conversion time – the time taken by the converter to convert the data and transmit it in the required form.

- The offset or compensation – for an input value of zero, the corresponding output should also be zero. Unfortunately this is not always the case: for a digital input of zero, the corresponding analogue voltage can be of the order of millivolts.
- The type of technology which can interface with the converter (TTL, CMOS, ECL etc).
- The accuracy – the difference between the value measured at the converter input and the value determined.
- The linearity between the input and output signals.
- The type of connection between the converter and the microprocessor system (see below).

According to the type of converter, two forms of connection with the microprocessor are possible as described in the following sections.

Converters connected directly to the system bus

Connection of the converter directly to the microprocessor bus (see Figs 4.42 and 4.43) is possible when the converter has a 'chip select' or 'chip enable' pin on the package; activation of this pin corresponds to the command to start conversion.

The main advantage of this type of connection is a reduction in cost and bulk since it is not necessary to use a parallel or serial peripheral interface device for the digital data in the converter. The disadvantage is that, if the device becomes defective, operation of the whole system can be affected.

Converters connected to a peripheral interface

Connection of the converter by way of a peripheral interface device (parallel or serial according to the type of converter) is shown in Figs 4.44 and 4.45.

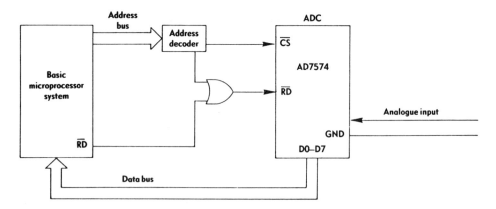

Figure 4.42 An 8-bit analogue-to-digital converter (AD 7574) connected to a microprocessor bus.

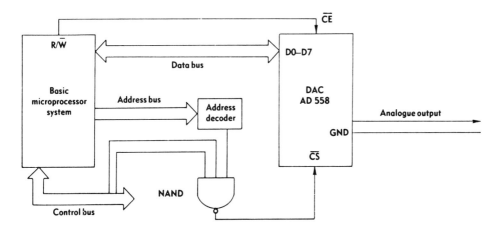

Figure 4.43 An 8-bit digital-to-analogue converter (AD 558) connected to a microprocessor bus.

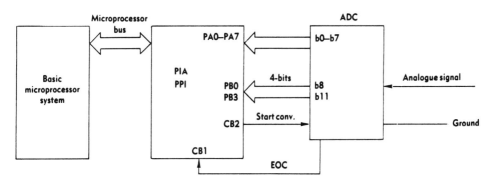

Figure 4.44 A 12-bit analogue-to-digital converter connected to a parallel interface device.

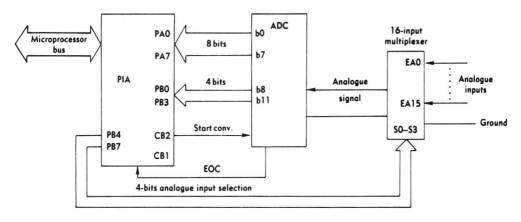

Figure 4.45 A multiplexed 12-bit analogue-to-digital converter connected to a parallel interface device.

4.15.6 Data Acquisition from Transducers

Transducers are used particularly in control and instrumentation and for the measurement and control of physical phenomena such as temperature, humidity, pressure, velocity and so on.

The choice of transducer depends on the following:

- The type of measurement to be made (temperature, pressure, humidity, velocity, counting, presence and movement detection of vehicles etc.)
- The minimum and maximum increments of the measured variable to be handled.

Acquisition of this type of measurement includes the following:

- Filtering of the transducer output signal to reduce the noise level with respect to the signal. Low-impedance connections are used and are formed from twisted pairs of wires or co-axial cables (see Fig. 4.46).

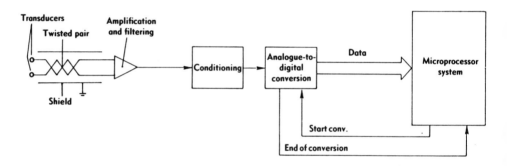

Figure 4.46 Acquisition and processing of a transducer signal with analogue conditioning.

- Amplification of the signal since the voltages provided by transducers are generally fairly low (for example, the output voltages of thermocouples vary from $-10\,mV$ to $10\,mV$).
- Conditioning – some values provided by the transducer do not reflect the actual physical value. To re-establish a correct scale of values, analogue (see Fig. 4.47) or digital techniques may be used.

In the case of digital conditioning, the analogue signal from the transducer is digitized using an analogue-to-digital converter (see page 115). Digital conditioning can be performed either by software, particularly in the case of products with a mathematical coprocessor, or by hardware using hard-wired digital electronic components.

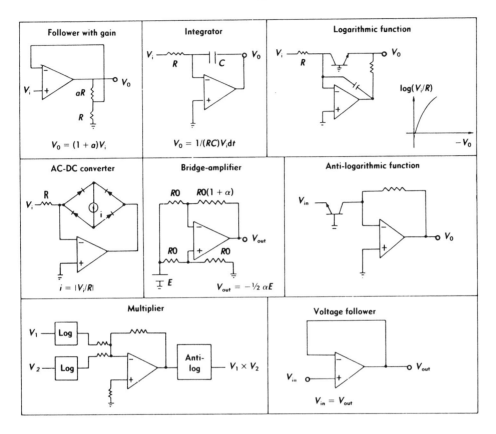

Figure 4.47 Outline diagrams of several analogue signal conditioning operations performed with circuits based on operational amplifiers.

4.15.7 Programmable Timers

The main function of a programmable timer is to generate one or more square waves of programmable frequency or a train of pulses conditioned by an external event. These signals can control one or more external circuits such as a loudspeaker (see Fig. 4.48). Examples of applications are pulse generators, frequency synthesizers, chronometers, frequency meters and so on.

4.16 Power Supplies for Microprocessor-based Products

Realization of the power supply starts by listing all the voltages required for correct operation of the various electronic components (both digital and analogue) and

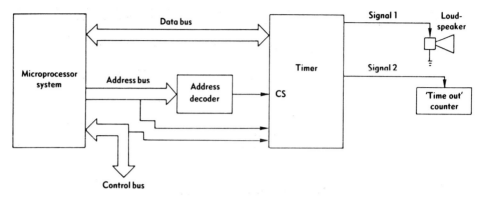

Figure 4.48 Block diagram for the connection of a timer circuit to a microprocessor bus.

other non-electronic (electromechanical) parts. The power at each of these voltages is the sum of the consumption of all the elements requiring this voltage.

Some products can be put into a stand-by mode; this state corresponds to a voluntary and selective removal of power. With the exception of certain 'sensitive' parts, all other parts of the product are not powered. Stand-by operation is found in communication, protection and security equipment and any other equipment which requires reduced energy consumption while ensuring continuous operation 24 hours per day.

Stand-by operation is initiated by a task of the lowest priority; this task tests whether any activity has been requested; if not, after a variable delay according to the product, stand-by operation of the product is initiated.

4.17   Breakdown Protection

Protection against breakdowns gives an important commercial advantage to the product. Only the simplest from a wide range of techniques will be described further. A 'protected' product enables an operator to recover work interrupted by a power failure or breakdown.

4.17.1   Power Failure

In a product which is protected against power failures, protection is achieved by saving the data for the process in progress during a power failure and restoring it when power returns.

It is necessary to include in the power supply a system which detects a fall in the supply used by the product (see Fig. 4.49); this involves provision of sufficient storage capacity in the supply and the use of a threshold detector.

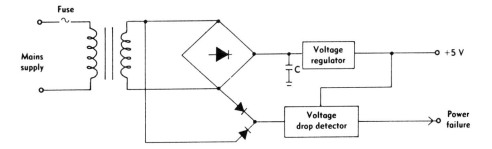

Figure 4.49 Block diagram of a power failure detection circuit.

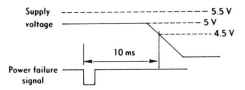

Figure 4.50 Power-failure detection: (a) supply voltage; (b) generation of a 'power-failure' pulse.

During very brief power failures, the charge stored in the capacitor is sufficient to power the circuits and recharging occurs between failures. In contrast, when a true power failure occurs, and the stored energy reaches a critical threshold, an alarm signal is activated (see Fig. 4.50). This signal requests the highest-priority interrupt which causes execution of a program to save the task in progress before halting the machine.

Comment Data are saved, during a power failure, in a memory which is protected against loss of voltage, for example NVRAM (see page 82).

The time for which power is maintained, after detection of a power failure, must be sufficient to perform the processing defined by the algorithm of Fig. 4.51. On the return of power, the system restores the context and returns control to the process which was interrupted by the power failure.

4.17.2 The 'Watch-dog' Technique

A watch-dog is a simple counter which must be re-initialized periodically by the program. If, at a given moment, a program being executed jams on one instruction,

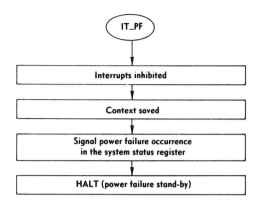

Figure 4.51 An example of processing during a power failure.

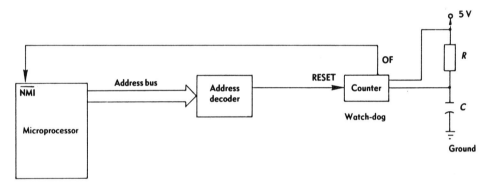

Figure 4.52 Block diagram for the connection of a 'watch-dog' to a microprocessor. When the counter reaches its maximum value, the following increment activates the overflow signal which can trigger a non-maskable interrupt signal.

the counter continues to increment; when it reaches its maximum value it generates an 'overflow' signal which initiates an interrupt (see Fig. 4.52), a RESET signal or some other strategy used by the product developer.

In this way, the watch-dog returns control to the user when operation of the product deteriorates without any attention or intervention. Depending on the product, the count duration of the watch-dog varies from 100 to 500 ms.

Note In a multiprocessor system, the role of the watch-dog can be filled by one or more microprocessors; this role can then extend to complex functions for controlling correct operation of the various microprocessors. If one breaks down, the watch-dog can request another microprocessor to fulfil the function of the defective microprocessor.

4.18   The Mother Board or Inter-board Bus

Interconnection of the various electronic cards used in the project requires the definition and installation of a bus between the cards; the definition provides the mechanical specification of the cards, maximum width and height, mounting, type of connector with the mother board etc., the various signals (data, address and control) and the physical location of each of these signals on the connectors between the mother and daughter boards. This location must be identical for all circuit boards; otherwise each card will have one unique location on the mother board (or backplane). In this case, to avoid putting a card in a location other than that provided for it, it is necessary to provide polarizing keys on one or more cards or to use connectors of different types on the mother board. This increases the cost of the development and particularly manufacturing phases.

The bus on the mother board contains all the signals required for correct operation of the functions available on the daughter boards; these signals are as follows:

- The data signals (those of the microprocessor data bus).
- The address signals (those of the microprocessor address bus).
- The control signals (all or part of the microprocessor control bus).
- The clock signals.
- The supply voltages for the various daughter boards.

The role of the mother board is to provide connection between the daughter boards; it is in the form of a card which contains all the connectors in which the various cards of the product will be located. Links are made by way of the bus interconnections of the various cards. The connection between the mother and daughter boards uses a male connector soldered on to the daughter boards which fits into one of the female connectors on the mother board.

The interconnecting bus, as defined above, can be standard or special. Each standard bus has specifications which define both its mechanical and electrical

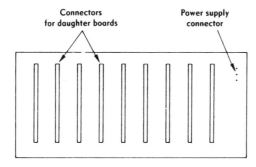

Figure 4.53 Mother board or interconnecting bus between the various cards. In the majority of cases, the connectors on the mother board are of the female type.

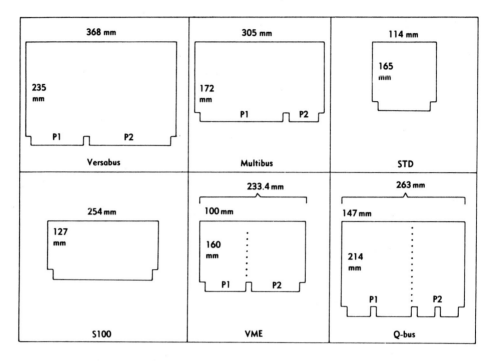

Figure 4.54 The form and characteristics of cards designed for standard buses.

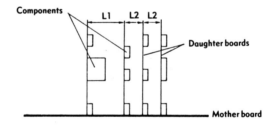

Figure 4.55 The separation between cards; during design of the mother board the maximum heights of the components on each card must be taken into account.

characteristics. Examples of standard buses (see Fig. 4.54) are VME, Multibus, PC-bus (IBM for the IBM-PC), STD, Versabus, Qbus and S100.

In certain cases it is necessary to provide a specific location for certain daughter boards, not because of the electrical signals on the bus, but to make efficient use of the distance separating cards from other cards. Certain components have a greater height than others; examples are relays and components which require a cooling device below the chip (see Fig. 4.55).

Note   The spacing between cards (see Fig. 4.55) must observe certain rules as
follows:

- The space varies according to the devices and products used (ECL, CMOS etc.);
  the inter-card distance is generally between 1.3 and 2 cm or more.
- A card containing devices which are a source of heat can affect the behaviour of
  components on other cards if sufficient separation is not provided.

4.19   Line Drivers

If the output signal of a chip feeds several packages (see Fig. 4.56), as is the case with
the data, address and control buses, its output power must be sufficient.

System bus drivers are therefore placed on each card in order to avoid any signal
degradation which could disturb the system.

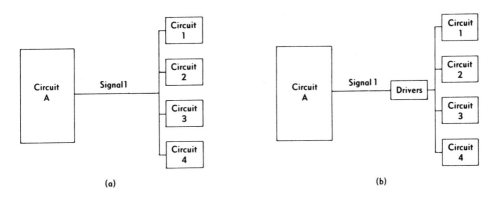

Figure 4.56 (a) The output signal of circuit A feeds several circuits simultaneously;
if it cannot support the load, circuits 1–4 may not operate correctly; (b) drivers
permit circuits 1– 4 to be driven by the signal from circuit A.

Printed Circuit Design

Since the introduction of computer-aided design (CAD) packages which operate on
dedicated workstations (such as MENTOR, DAISY and Computervision),
minicomputers (such as VAX and HP 9000) and microcomputers, the time required
for printed circuit design and its cost have been considerably reduced. The
processing power and the facilities available on these systems vary enormously.
Another advantage of CAD is the possibility of reusing the data for one product in
the later stages of development of a new product.

4.20   Stages in the Design of a Printed Circuit

Computer-aided design (CAD) can be used to create the required printed circuits (the mother board, the daughter boards and the power-supply card). As a first step, the following information should be provided:

- An inventory of the active and passive components, and connectors with details of package identification, size, form and number of pins for each. This list enables the total component and connector area on each card to be determined.
- A schematic diagram of each card used including a detailed description of the various interconnections between the components for each card.
- A drawing of the card which enables the dimensions of the card and the useful area available for mounting components to be determined.
- The location of the connectors and identification of the signals on the connector pins.

This information provides the data which can be used by the CAD system to design the printed circuits. Production of printed circuit boards using CAD tools can be internal or subcontracted to specialist companies.

The design of printed circuit boards involves the following stages (see Fig. 4.57):

- Obtaining the data: all the data mentioned above is fed into the CAD database.
- Checking the schematic diagrams.

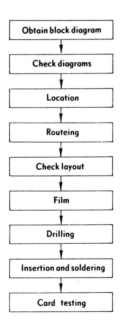

Figure 4.57 Stages in the design of a printed circuit.

- Testing the card by simulation; the simulation can test both logic and timing.
- Laying out the various components on the card. The CAD program locates the components by similarity of type (analogue-to-digital converters, memories etc.) but leaves the user free to move components to other locations.
- Routeing of the interconnections between the packages and between the packages and the connectors on the card. Routeing can be made at one or more levels (by using multilayer boards) and must observe the rules associated with fabrication constraints (the size of tracks, the separation of tracks, etc.).
- Checking the correct route of tracks and interconnections.
- Fabricating the printed card.
- Drilling.
- Inserting and soldering the components onto the printed card.
- Card testing; during card testing (see page 157), it should be noted that all faults detected (badly mounted components, poor soldering etc.) can recur. It is therefore recommended that these faults are reported to the production line in order to avoid recurrence and to improve production quality.

Note In certain cases, depending on the infrastructure of the organization, the operations of fabrication of the printed card, drilling, component insertion and soldering can be contracted out (see Fig. 4.57).

The choice of CAD system, when printed circuit production is not contracted out, is determined by particular features of the product together with the following:

- The card density: the CAD system can be single or multilayer and the maximum number of layers must be defined.
- The types of package to be used: surface mounted components, single in-line packages (SIP), hybrid circuits etc.
- The mode of component insertion: for example, components on both faces of the printed board.
- The rate of automatic routeing.
- The need to process both digital and analogue cards.
- The amount and type of information contained in the CAD system library.
- Documentation: the facility to support text processing which can be included in electronic schematics.

High-speed integrated circuits impose constraints on the geometry of connectors and the size and spacing of connecting lines. These constraints are due to cross-talk of the digital signals associated with spurious inductance and capacitance which can degrade the operation of electronic components. This type of problem can be alleviated by:

- Interleaving the signal lines and power supply and earth buses; this permits the capacitive effects between signals to be reduced.
- Increasing the distances between signals on the printed circuit boards.
- Avoiding parallel signals over long distances.

Note 1 The increased integration density of chips, particularly for microprocessors, involves an increase in the number of pins per chip and a consequent increase of interconnection density. This increase will, eventually, influence printed circuit technology, the design tools used and the types of packaging used for one or more devices in distinct modules.

Note 2 The connector types, their disposition on the cards and the arrangement of card guides must be such as to avoid damage to connector pins when inserting cards. Excessive pressure on the part of the operator inserting the cards should be avoided.

Note 3 In the case of military or vehicle-mounted hardware the following should be provided:

- Adequate clearance between cards.
- A mechanical system for clamping cards in their guides and connectors; this limits the effects of vibration as far as possible.
- Connectors with supports for clamps and contacts of a type which ensure sufficient pressure to avoid separation of the contacts due to vibration.

4.21 Package Types

The form of the integrated circuit package together with the arrangement, separation and number of pins is called the 'packaging'. The package material is either plastic characterized by operating specifications to civil standards (permitted temperature range 0–70°C), or ceramic characterized by operating specifications to military standards (temperature range −55–125°C).

For a given chip, ceramic encapsulation costs more than plastic; up to 40 pins, the price ratio of ceramic DIP packages to plastic DIP packages is around 6. This ratio falls to 3 for a number of pins greater than 40. For 'chip carrier' packages, the ceramic/plastic price ratio is around 4.

Soldering an integrated circuit onto a printed circuit card can be achieved either by insertion or by surface mounting depending on the device (see Fig. 4.58).

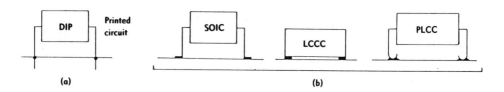

(a)   (b)

Figure 4.58 The two ways of mounting integrated circuits on a printed circuit board: (a) mounting by insertion for a DIP; (b) surface mounting for a small outline integrated circuit (SOIC), a leadless ceramic chip carrier (LCCC) and a plastic leaded chip carrier (PLCC).

Packages can be of the following types:

- Dual-in-line package (DIP): the pins are arranged on two sides and the pin separation is 2.54 mm.
- Shrink DIP: the pins are arranged on two sides and the pin separation is 1.78 mm,
- Skinny DIP.
- Single-in-line package (SIP): the pins are arranged on one side only; the main advantage is a useful gain in the space occupied by the device.
- Zig-zag in-line package (ZIP): a narrow package with the pins in two alternate rows, the separation is 2.54 mm.
- Small outline: a package with short conductors on two sides, the separation is 1.27 mm. It is located on the printed circuit card by surface mounting (see Fig. 4.58 and Table 4.6).

Table 4.6   The form of some integrated circuit packages.

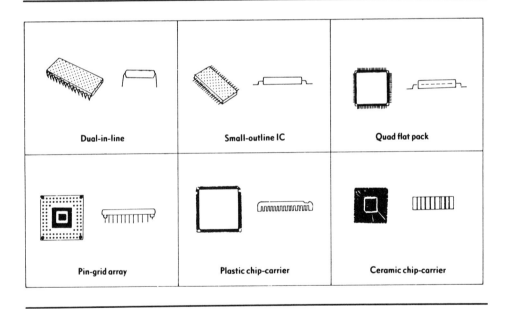

| Dual-in-line | Small-outline IC | Quad flat pack |
| Pin-grid array | Plastic chip-carrier | Ceramic chip-carrier |

- Pin grid array: a square package with pins on all four sides in two rows; the separation is 2.54 mm.
- Chip carrier: a square package with short pins on all four sides; the separation is 1.27 mm. It is located on the printed circuit card by surface mounting (see Fig. 4.58 and Table 4.6).

Test Accessories

Three types of accessory are required at the test and maintenance stage as discussed in Sections 4.22–24.

4.22   Extender Cards

An extender card is necessary when mechanical constraints prevent introduction of the emulation probe into the prototype (see page 157). The extender card is used during card testing, software/hardware integration, product validation and qualification (see Fig. 4.59).

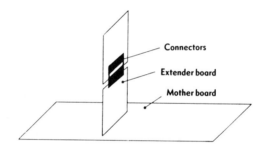

Figure 4.59 The use of an extender board.

4.23   Fault Indicators

The inclusion of easily visible LEDs to indicate errors on cards helps after-sales service by rapidly locating a defective card (see Fig. 4.60) and detecting the unit to be changed in the case of breakdown.

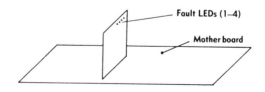

Figure 4.60 LED failure indicators.

Examples of indicators are:

- LED1: Bus inactive.
- LED2: DMA active.
- LED3: NMI active (non-maskable interrupt).
- LED4: IRQ inactive (maskable interrupt).

4.24 Test Points

Test points can be included on cards (see Fig. 4.61); these test points are pins which permit a probe to be connected, from a logic analyser for example. Signals from the card are brought out to these test points; signals must be chosen judiciously in terms of their importance and their role in the operation of the card.

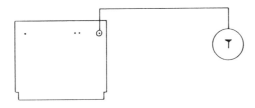

Figure 4.61 Test points on a card.

Chapter 5

Development Systems

Introduction

5.1 Historical

Since the invention of the planar transistor in 1959, the complexity of electronic systems and the density of integration of electronic components have increased considerably.

In the 1960s, the most dense components contained scarcely a thousand transistors; today, 16- and 32-bit microprocessors and 16-million-bit RAMs can contain several hundreds of thousands of transistors on the same chip.

This development directly affects the engineer as indicated in the following sections.

5.1.1 The Approach

In the 1960s, the engineer's attention would be devoted to the logic itself and the interconnections between devices. In the 1970s it would be devoted to software and the problems of architecture development.

In the 1980s, attention is directed very much towards the 'top-down' approach; that is, mastery of the operational details of the devices used (at least the most important ones such as microprocessors, clock circuits, gate arrays, custom chips, RAMs and peripheral interfaces). At the same time a thorough knowledge of microprocessor-based systems (particularly 8-bit ones) and minicomputer architecture is required, since some parts of the architecture of 32-bit micro-processors are similar to the operating structures of minicomputers.

5.1.2 The Tools

The tools used to design electronic systems have evolved with the new technology as shown in Fig. 5.1.

132

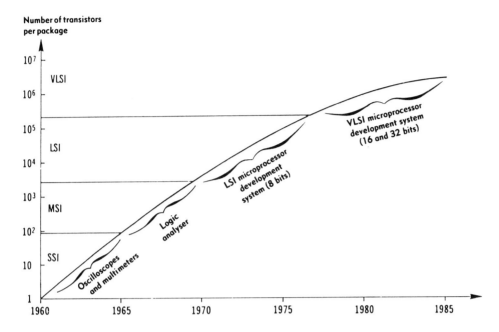

Figure 5.1 The increase in density of integration and its effect on the tools used for debugging electronic products.

Oscilloscopes and multimeters were adequate for development of products based on small-scale integrated circuits (SSI). Circuits based on medium-scale integration (MSI) required logic analysers. Microprocessor-based systems (large- or very large-scale integrated circuit devices (LSI) or (VLSI)) have contributed to the birth and evolution of development systems together with various utilities and aids necessary for the design of such systems.

The emergence of special-purpose integrated circuits (custom ICs) (which represented 30% of the semiconductor design market at the start of the 1980s and are expected to take 50% of the market by 1990), multiprocessor systems with parallel architecture (see Chapters 2 and 4) together with research and development in microprocessor architecture (for example RISC architecture) and software will make a substantial impact on the development tools of the 1990s.

5.2 Introduction to Development Systems

The evolution of integrated circuit technology has made the development system necessary and fundamental to every realization of a microprocessor-based electronic prototype.

Development systems include a number of features which provide substantial

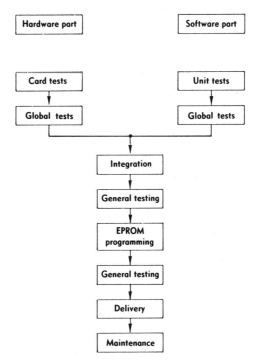

Figure 5.2 Block diagram of the development stages of a microprocessor-based product.

assistance to software and hardware designers during the whole period of design and commissioning of a microprocessor-based electronic prototype. Commissioning involves loading the program into the read only memory of the prototype and operating it in the environment for which it has been produced. It should be noted that many of the features of the development system are found in the majority of microcomputers on the market (examples are: a text-editing utility, compilers, an assembler, a directory manager, a linkage editor, memory assignment procedures, a debugger etc.)

During realization of a microprocessor-based product, two sections are realized separately – the software (see Chapter 3) and the hardware (see Chapter 4). Once these two sections are realized, the following steps are required (see Fig. 5.2):

- Test each part separately (unit and global tests).
- If required, modify the source programs due to the detection of software errors.
- Regenerate executable code.
- Load the software into the electronic hardware (integration).
- Test the whole product including the software and the hardware (dynamic testing).
- Program the EPROMs when the software and hardware have been tested.

The development system is used for all the stages indicated in Fig. 5.2. It serves the following purposes:

- Software realization (see Fig. 5.7):

  ★ Creation and modification of source programs with the help of a text editing utility.
  ★ Compilation or assembly of the source programs to generate the object files.
  ★ Execution of the linkages between modules using a linkage editing utility.
  ★ Assignment of user defined memory areas by means of the 'LOCATE' memory assignment utility.

- Software testing:

  ★ Execution of unit and global tests by means of the debugging utility.

- Hardware testing:

  ★ Creation of a set of test programs (a 'battery of tests') for devices and electronic cards using the utilities mentioned in (a) and the emulation pod which will be described later in this chapter.

- Integration of the software and hardware:

  ★ Integration of the software and hardware and testing of the resulting combination using the emulation utility in conjunction with the emulation pod.

- Programming read only memories (EPROM and PROM):

  ★ Programming of EPROM and PROM using the read only memory programming tools available in the development system.

- General Testing:

  ★ Test the whole product with the executable program incorporated in the read only memory of the prototype by means of the emulation pod and utility.

- Product maintenance through 'after-sales service'

  ★ Maintenance can also be supported by the development system either by emulation (using the pod and emulation utility) or by a specific maintenance program.

The basic development system is in the form of a microcomputer which has the following facilities (see Fig. 5.3):

- A set of peripherals (screen, keyboard, printer, floppy disk drive, hard disk).
- An assembly of electronic cards; these cards, which will be described in this chapter, in conjunction with the development system software form the resources used for the design and commissioning of the prototype.
- An emulation pod.

Development systems have greatly increased the speed of microprocessor-based

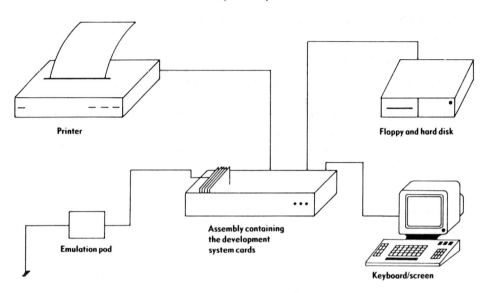

Figure 5.3 The development system and its peripherals.

product design. The aids provided by development systems are intended for both software designers and electronic engineers. They are very powerful tools which are necessary for the creation of every microprocessor-based application.

5.2.1 Types of Development System

Four types of development system are available on the market, as follows:

Systems specific to standard microprocessors

These are systems dedicated to a single microprocessor family and provided by the component manufacturer. In general they are available quickly. As it is designed by the microprocessor manufacturer, the system is often available at the same time as the commercial launch of the microprocessor itself. The availability of a good development system is one of the key factors in the successful sale of a new microprocessor.

Examples of specific development systems are as follows:

- The Motorola EXORCISER for the M6800 family (8 bits).
- The Motorola EXORMAC for the M68000 family (16 bits).
- The Intel INTELLEC series for the 8080/8085/8086/8087/8088/80186/80188/80286 family.

- The Intel iPDS for the 8080/8085 family (a portable development system).
- The Zilog ZSCAN 8000 for the Z8000 family.

Systems specific to custom microprocessors

These are development systems provided by the manufacturers of custom micro-processors and microcontrollers. These systems are comparable, in functional terms, to systems specific to standard microprocessors.

Semi-universal systems

These systems support two or more microprocessors from different manufacturers; however, the microprocessors concerned have comparable internal architectures and, particularly, instruction sets.

An example is a development system for 8080, 8085 and Z80 microprocessors; there is upward compatibility in the instruction sets of these three microprocessors from different manufacturers (Intel and Zilog).

Universal development systems

Universal development systems are intended to support all types of microprocessor on the market; unfortunately they fail to do this. In fact universal development systems, in response to demand, support the most widely available microprocessors on the market. Consequently, the delays in the appearance of such systems on the market are much greater than those of specific systems. Universal development systems are designed by specialized instrument manufacturers such as Tektronix, Hewlett-Packard and Philips. They support the most widely used microprocessors such as the products of Motorola, Intel and Zilog.

Examples of universal development systems are:

- The Tektronix 8001/8002 and 8560.
- The Hewlett-Packard HP 64100A.
- The Philips PM4421 (single user) and PM4422 (multi-user).
- The Gould Millennium 9516S.
- The Microtek MPDS.
- The Hilevel Technology DS370 and DS3700 (specially for bit-slice micro-processors).

Note   Some universal development systems are also available for IBM PCs and compatibles such as:

- The Microtek MICE.
- The Emulogic SLICE with the DE-1000 emulator.
- The KONTRON KSE.
- The Step Engineering Step-27 and Step-40 (for bit-slice microprocessors).

5.3   Choice of Development System Type

5.3.1   Choice with Respect to Use

Although development systems generally have the same hardware and software tools, it is important to match the hardware and software requirements of the project (utilities, languages etc.) to the available facilities and documentation of the development system.

The availability of, and time required for, software and hardware maintenance are also factors which must be taken into account; these factors have an enormous influence on the time required to realize the product (see Chapter 6).

The choice from the models available will be influenced by the following:

- The type of microprocessor selected during the software/hardware division phase (see Chapter 2).
- Whether development work is to involve one or more types of microprocessor. If this has not been determined, it is important to do so quickly in order to avoid superfluous medium- and long-term investment. A specific development system is suitable for one type of microprocessor, a universal system for several.
- Whether the organization has anticipated the use of a standard bus type. If it has, many development facilities, particularly electronic circuit cards, will be available: examples are the Intel Multibus and the Motorola VME bus.
- Whether or not the organization has expertise with a particular type of microprocessor; if not, provision must be made for the following:

  - The training budget.
  - The time required to acquire 'know how'.
  - The resultant delay in realizing the project.

All the above factors must be taken into account in the time required to realize the prototype.

- The availability from the development system supplier of a library of programs together with software and hardware application notes. These can save an appreciable amount of time in running the project; some of these notes can be utilized for the project itself.
- The facilities for linking and interfacing with minicomputers available in the organization (see Fig. 5.4); this is an important factor with large projects. The minicomputer must permit the following:

  - Transfer of program files and documentation from the minocomputer to the development system and vice versa.
  - Acquisition of project documentation (thereby relieving the load on the development system terminals).
  - Version management for the whole project.
  - General archiving.
  - Software development on the minicomputer when a development system terminal is not available.

- Whether the designer is, or is not, associated with a particular manufacturer.
- Particular cases (in military applications, for example, the Motorola MC6800 was available in a military version long before other microprocessors of comparable power).

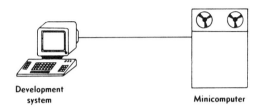

Development
system   Minicomputer

Figure 5.4 A development system connected to a minicomputer.

5.3.2   The Cost

Universal development systems are much more expensive than specific ones. Before purchasing, it is recommended that an evaluation should be made of all the facilities and tools which will be required throughout the project.

5.3.3   Multi-user Systems

Some types of universal and specific development system offer a multi-user facility. Examples are the Intel Intellec with the Network Development System (NDS) and the Philips PM4422.

Multi-user systems are generally required for large projects where it is necessary to provide several workstations (see Fig. 5.5). In this case, procedures and strict discipline for periodically saving files and managing different versions of the software and documentation are required.

The advantages of multi-user systems are as follows:
The resources of a central development site can be used by several people at the same time (the mass memory capacity for file creation is greater), and common resources such as a printer can be shared. A direct consequence is a reduction in the cost of each workstation.

The disadvantages of multi-user systems are as follows:
Problems can arise with management of software versions from different programmers and programming teams. These can create technical and human problems which can delay the project dramatically.

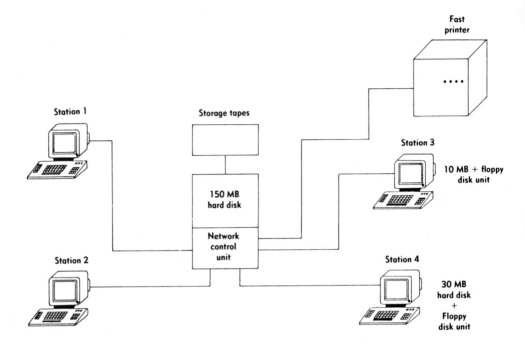

Figure 5.5 A network of development systems.

There are two types of multi-user configuration:

Multi-user systems with a shared central processing unit. All terminals are connected to a single central processing unit which undertakes all work requested by each terminal connected to the network; an example is the Tektronix 8560. The disadvantages of systems of this type are the response time, which increases with the number of terminals connected to the network, and the possibility of breakdown of the central processing unit which will involve breakdown of all the terminals. The advantage is a relatively large reduction in the cost per station.

Multi-user systems with distributed processing power. Each terminal has a central processing unit which permits local processing while accessing common resources (particularly the mass memory and the printer); an example is the Intel NDS development system.

The advantages lie where systems with a shared central processor have their weaknesses; response times are not affected by the number of stations and a breakdown of the central processing unit does not halt all the terminals. The disadvantage is that the cost per station is greater than that of systems with shared central processing.

The Elements of a Development System _____

The tools provided by a development system are essentially dedicated to the development of microprocessor-based applications. These tools may be separated into two main sections – software and hardware.

5.4   Software Elements

It should be noted that the majority of software elements are, to a large extent, found in every microcomputer operating system on the market, so learning will be relatively easy for anyone who is familiar with computing techniques.

To design a program which can be loaded into the memory of a microcomputer, it is necessary to follow a sequence of steps which are similar for every development system (see Fig. 5.7). This is achieved with the help of a set of utilities.

The utilities contained in a development system can be divided into seven groups as follows:

- Directory and common resource management utilities.
- Text-editing and language utilities.
- System utilities.
- Linkage editing utilities.
- Memory assignment or 'mapping' utilities.
- Debugging utilities.
- Read only memory programming utilities.

The goal of all these utilities is to generate a program which is executable, tested and can be loaded into the read only memory of the prototype.

The design of a loadable program makes use of the following:

- A personal directory which is assigned to the user and is protected from access by a password. (This directory is generally assigned by the software development or project manager.)
- A text-editing utility which permits creation, modification and saving of source files (program files in assembler or other higher-level language) or documents.
- Programming language utilities which compile and generate object and list files.
- A linkage editing utility which combines the object files and resolves calls to procedures and external data defined in the various program files.
- A utility which permits the user to define the memory map in agreement with the system designer.
- A utility for loading and debugging the executable program on the development system; this gives the program its definitive form.

5.4.1   Utilities for Directory and Common Resource Management

When stations are connected to a network, it is fundamentally important that each team or individual has a personal directory. Common files are protected by the project leader against any deletion or modification.

LOGON: Gives the user access to the common resources of a network from his terminal. This access is personalized by name; this name limits access by the operator to files contained in his directory and prohibits access by him to other protected directories unless he knows the name of the directory and its password. This permits accidental modifications to be avoided (for example, use, deletion or modification of files which the operator should not possess).

```
=LOGON
DIRECTORY'S NAME? MAIN
PASSWORD?####
=
```

Access to the MAIN directory is protected by a password.

LOGOFF: Disconnects the workstation from the network. When the user executes this command, the only resources at his disposal are those contained on the floppy and hard disks of his own station.

```
=LOGOFF
```

Station disconnected from the network.

Note – Conventions

- The '=' character indicates to the user that he is under system control and can input a development system command from the keyboard.
- The '?' or '*' character indicates to the user that he is under the control of a system utility component. The only commands permitted are those recognized by the utility (for example, the 'LIB' utility which permits program libraries to be generated).
- The '*' character is a wild card; it serves as a substitute for any set of characters.
- Characters enclosed by the ':' character represent the name of a peripheral. For example, ':CON:' corresponds to the display, the system identifies it by 'CON' which is an abbreviation for 'CONSOLE'. These names are those given by the system itself.

5.4.2   Text-editing and Language Utilities

Text editors
These serve to create and modify source programs from the keyboard. The majority of development system text editors have the following functions:

> Vertical movement of the text on the screen, movement of the cursor to the left, right, up and down, copying blocks of text into the same or several documents, searching for strings of characters, partial or total replacement of one character set file by another, input/output with or without saving the edited file, the facility to create editing macros to perform several editing commands at once, the facility to display lines of more than 80 characters. The main differences between available text editors occur in their ease of use.

Compilers (see Chapter 3)
These serve to transform source programs into object code programs with an indication of syntax errors in the source programs. Examples of language compilers are Pascal, PLM86, C, ADA etc.

Assemblers (see Chapter 3)
The assemblers available on development systems are those for the microprocessors which the system can emulate (the emulation function will be treated later in this chapter).

Interpreter: BASIC
Because of its convenience, this language can be used in certain hardware-testing programs and in the creation of specific software tools to permit some parts to be operated during development.

5.4.3   System Utilities

These are the most substantial, in quantitative terms, utilities of a development system. The names given to these utilities in this book are arbitrary, they can be found under different names according to the particular development system, while still having the same functions as those which are described below.

Most of the list cited below will be familiar to the reader; some systems also have other utilities which facilitate the task of the developer, for example:

- A utility for managing and generating versions.
- A MAIL utility for intergroup co-ordination and communication, receiving and sending messages or files using personalized mailboxes for the various directories.
- A utility for linking the development system to a minicomputer.

FORMAT: This permits formatting a hard or floppy disk with the possibility of including the operating system and/or assigning a name to the disk.

```
=FORMAT :FO:TEST S
Insert new diskette for drive 0
and type (CR) key when ready
or type (END) to quit          CR
formatting..........format complete
system transferred
Format another (Y/N)?N
=
```

System formatting (by means of the parameter *S*) of the diskette placed in unit FO; this disk will carry the name 'TEST'; the system files are automatically transferred to the diskette.

COPY: This permits duplication of files.

```
=COPY :FO:PROGCL24.P86 TO :F1:PROGCL24.P86
COPIED :FO:PROGCL24.P86 TO :F1:PROGCL24.P86
=
```

Duplication of the file PROGCL24.P86 contained in physical unit FO to physical unit F1. If the file already exists in F1, the system displays a message indicating this and requests the user to confirm duplication and overwriting of the file already existing in unit F1.

TYPE: Permits the contents of a file to be displayed on the screen.

```
=TYPE  :FO:DOCARCHI.V00
```

Display the file DOCARCHI.V00 contained on the diskette in unit FO on the screen. This command can be replaced by the command 'COPY:F0:DOCARCHI.V00 TO :CON:', where CON is the name corresponding to the screen.

PRINT: Prints a document.

```
=PRINT :FO:DOCARCHI.V00
NAME OF LIST DEVICE [SPL]:
RESIDENT PART OF PRINT INSTALLED
PROGTX.SRC       IS CURRENTLY BEING PRINTED
DOCARCHI.V00 IS IN QUEUE
=
```

Prints the document DOCARCHI.V00 on the diskette in unit F0. If a 'spooler' is installed, the above command can be replaced by 'COPY:F0:: DOCHARCHI.V00 to :SPL:', where SPL is the name given to the printer queue.

DIR: Permits the contents or 'index' of a floppy disk, hard disk or a directory to be displayed. This display is accompanied by type information: length, date of creation of the file and an indicator to show whether the file is protected or not.

```
=DIR 1
DIRECTORY DEVELOP
NAME       .EXT      SIZE      LENGTH      ATTR

MONITV3  .A86        30        3690
GLIGNE    .PAS       237       29151        W
GLIGNE    .OBJ       102       12546        W
GLIGNEV3 .PAS       247       30381
GLIGNEV3 .OBJ       106       13038
GLIGNEV3 .LST        439       53997
=
```

In the example above all the files contained in physical unit F1 with the suffices (or extensions) of each file, the number of blocks in each, the length in bytes and the attributes of each one are listed. Several options generally accompany this command, such as display only of the names of files with their suffices or display and creation of a file containing a list of the files contained in the unit.

NAME (or RENAME): Permits the name of one or more files to be changed (the wild card character '*' is used by almost all manufacturers; it replaces a string of characters).

```
=RENAME PROGV2.5SC TO PROGV3.OSC
=
```

Changing the name of file PROGV2.5SC to PROGV3.0SC.

DEL: Deletion of one or more files.

```
=DEL DOC*.V25 C
DELETE DOCSGF.V25 (Y/N)?Y
DOCSGF.V25 DELETED
DELETE DOCVISU.V25 (Y/N)?N

DELETE DOCMONIT.V25 (Y/N)?Y
DOCMONIT.V25 DELETED
=
```

Deletion of all files whose names begin with DOC and have the suffix V25 with confirmation of each deletion (by means of the parameter C in the command).

ASSIGN: Permits a physical unit to be assigned to a logical unit.

```
=ASSIGN 1 TO /MAIN/EFIRM/
=
```

For example, the file FLOPD.PAS contained in the directory /MAIN/EFIRM can be referenced in the form ':F1:FLOPD.PAS'

DATETIME: A utility to update the system date and time; the index file assigns a date and time to files contained in the mass memories of the development system.

```
=DATETIME
DATE(11/29/82)? 12/25/85
TIME(11-30-00)? 08-20-00
=
```

Creating and starting a BATCH file   An ASCII file containing a set of commands is created by the text-editing utility. On starting this BATCH file, the system executes each of the commands contained in it. In certain cases, the same function can be provided by a file called 'SUBMIT'.

Example: The contents of the file BATCH 'GENFWV3.BAT' or SUBMIT 'GENFWV3.CSD'

```
=TYPE GENFWV3.BAT
ASM MONITV3.ASM
ASM CLAVV3.ASM
PASCAL GLIGNEV3.PAS CODE
COPY *.LST TO :SPL:
DEL *.LST
LINK MONITV3.OBJ CLAVV3.OBJ GLIGNEV3.OBJ TO MODFIRM.LNK
=
```

The first two lines call for assembly of two files; the third line calls for Pascal compilation of the file GLIGNEV3.PAS with generation of an assembler list file. This if followed by printing before deletion of all files with the suffix 'LST' and finally linkage editing of the files MONITV3.OBJ, CLAVV3.OBJ and GLIGNE.OBJ.

ATTRIB: Permits files to be protected against accidental deletion or modification or made invisible to the user (for example, they are not displayed during execution of the 'DIR' command).

```
=ATTRIB :FO:GTRANS*.SRC W

    FILE                     CURRENT ATTRIBUTE
 :FO:GTRANS2.SRC                     W
 :FO:GTRANS1.SRC                     W
 =
```

All files whose names start with GTRANS and have a suffix 'SRC' will be write protected.

DISKCOPY: Duplication of the contents of a hard disk to another hard disk or magnetic tape.

```
=DISKCOPY 1 TO 0
LOAD DISK(S), THEN TYPE (CR)
DRIVE 1 IS SOURCE DISK
DRIVE 0 DISK WILL BE OVERWRITTEN
TYPE Y TO CONFIRM OR N TO RESUME?
Y
*************************************************
*************************************************
**************************************
DRIVE 1 DISK COPIED TO DRIVE 0
VERIFY OK
DISK COPY COMPLETED
=
```

BACKUP: Total or partial saving of a floppy or hard disk.

```
=BACKUP 0 TO HD0
Insert backup hard disk 0
Warning! files in hard disk 0 will be destroyed
Strike (CR) key when ready        CR
Insert backup hard disk in drive 0
Strike (CR) key when ready
*****Backing up files to hard disk 0****
ADOC2.DOC
ADOCUSYS.DOC
ALTRANS.DOC
AXPORT2.DOC
.
.
.
XPHILV25.DOC
=
```

Saving of all the files contained in unit 0 on unit HD0.

RESTORE: Restoration of saved files on to the working unit (floppy or hard disk).

```
=RESTORE HD0 TO 0
Insert backup hard disk 0
Strike (CR) key when ready
*****Restoring files from hard disk 0****
ADOC2.DOC
ADOCUSYS.DOC
ALTRANS.DOC
AXPORT2.DOC
.
.
.
XPHILV25.DOC
=
```

Restoration of all the files previously saved on HD0 to physical unit 0.

InstallQM: Permits installation of queue administration, which is particularly necessary for the spooler. The 'InstallQM' and 'InstallSPL' commands are, in general, the first commands executed by the operator after powering up the development system.

```
=INSTALLQM
QUEUE MANAGER INSTALLED
=
```

InstallSPL: Permits installation of the printer in spooler mode.

```
=INSTALLSPL
SPOOLER INSTALLED
=
```

SPOOLER: The command to access the spooler. This command permits display of the names and lengths of files which are awaiting printing in the spooler queue. This command also permits removal of files from the queue and display of error messages related to printing files (for example, 'out of paper', 'printer disconnected' etc.).

REPAIR: Permits testing or recovery of files on a diskette on which some sectors are corrupted.

```
=REPAIR :FO:
```

On execution of this command, the user can list the bad sectors together with their number. These sectors can be modified or excluded from later access.

LIB: Permits the user to create or modify a library of programs (by deletion or addition of a module) with the facility of displaying information on each module contained in the library such as the date of creation, the public procedures and the segments.

```
=LIB
SYSTEM  SC  LIBRARIAN  V2.1
?CREATE COMM.LIB
?ADD  GLIGNE.OBJ  CTRANSP.OBJ  CAPPLI.OBJ
?LIST COMM.LIB
GESLIGNE
COTRANSP
COAPPLIC
?DELETE  COMM.LIB  CAPPLI.OBJ
?LIST  COMM.LIB
GESLIGNE
COTRANSP
?QUIT
=
```

In this example, a library 'COMM.LIB' is created which contains the modules GLIGNE.OBJ, CTRANSP.OBJ and CAPPLI.OBJ. The command 'LIST' indicates the three modules contained in the library COMM.LIB; these three names correspond to the names of the modules contained at the start of the three source programs. The DELETE command enables the module CAPPLI.OBJ to be deleted from the library 'COMM.LIB'.

CONVOH: Permits an absolute object module to be converted into an object module in hexadecimal format.

```
=CONVOH COMDAT.OBJ TO COMDAT.HEX
=
```

CONVHO: Permits an object module in hexadecimal format to be converted into an absolute object module.

```
=CONVHO COMDAT.HEX TO COMDAT.OBJ
=
```

LOAD: Loads an executable program into memory and gives control to this program.

```
=LOAD GESCOM.LOD
?
```

Loading of an executable program GESCOM.LOD into the development system memory.

5.4.4 The Linkage Editor Utility

The linkage editor permits modularization of programs (see page 58). After the compiler has transformed a source module into an object module, the linkage editor enables the following to be performed:

- Linking of the object modules in the order defined by their programmer.
- Recombination (by linking) of object modules compiled independently; the linkages are determined by references made from one program to another.

```
=LINK :F1:MONITV3.OBJ, :F3:GLIGNE.OBJ, :F1:CLAVV3.OBJ,§
        :F3:GTRANSP.OBJ, :F4:GSESSION.OBJ   TO :F2:GCOMV3.LNK

Linker Version 2.0 (C) Copyright XXXXX 1985

Unresolved externals

TO_TRX86 in file(s):
GLIGNE.OBJ (GESLIGNE)

There was 1          error(s) detected
=
```

In the example above, linkage editing is performed for modules :F1: MONITV3.OBJ, :F3:GLIGNE.OBJ, :F1:CLAVV3.OBJ, :F3:GTRANSP.OBJ and :F4:GSESSION.OBJ; this utility establishes the linkages between all elements, such as procedures, declared as external by any modules. If one or more procedures or variables are declared external in any module and are defined neither in any of the modules included in the linkage editing nor in the library of references, an error message is displayed on the screen and included in the file which is created automatically during each linkage editing. The procedures or symbols not defined will be listed under the heading 'names of undefined externals'.

The linkage editor must provide the facility of calling up user libraries which are consulted during linkage editing. Other options can also be available such as the option to generate an executable file in addition to the linkage editing.

An example of the execution of a linkage between two modules is shown at the top of p. 152.

During linkage editing, the name of the procedure 'PRINT-MSG', declared as external and called by the procedure 'TEST-LINE' of program A, will be noted in the symbol table; the linkage editor establishes the link between the calling procedure 'TEST-LINE' and the called procedure 'PRINT-MSG' of programs A and B.

5.4.5   Memory Map Definition Utility

This permits the user to assign absolute addresses to the relative addresses of modules; this assignment enables the available memory areas to be distributed; for example, the code part is assigned to the ROM and the data part to the RAM. It also permits the memory map to be displayed including the start of the code, the data and stack pointer address areas and the size of each.

Program A   **Program B**

```
.
.
.
Print_Msg: Procedure (msg) External;
   DECLARE msg Byte;
End Print_Msg;
.
.
.
.
Test_Line: Procedure (p_arg, s_type)
                        Reentrant;
   DECLARE p_arg Pointer,
              .
              .
      .
      .
   CALL Print_Msg (message);
      .
      .
End Test-Line;
```

```
.
.
.
.
.
.
Print_Msg: Procedure (msg) Public;
   DECLARE msg Byte,
              rang Word;
.
.
.
.
   rang=rang+1;
.
.
End Print_Msg;
.
.
.
.
.
.
```

In the following example, the code is located starting at address 2000H and the data starting at address 5000H.

```
=LOCATE MODCOM.LINK TO MODCOM.LOC §
ADDRESSES(                          §
          CLASSES(                  §
               CODE(02000H),        §
               DATA(05000H)))       §

Locater Version 2.0 (C) Copyright XXXXX 1985
```

Several options are generally possible, such as the order of storing the various segments and a choice of the address of the first instruction to be executed in the program generated.

5.4.6 The Executable Program Debugging Utility

The debugging utility is a tool which facilitates testing for errors in executable software. The debugger overlaps very much with the emulation function (see page

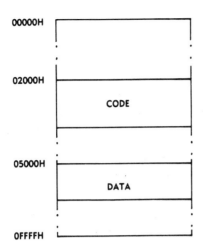

Figure 5.6 Memory map.

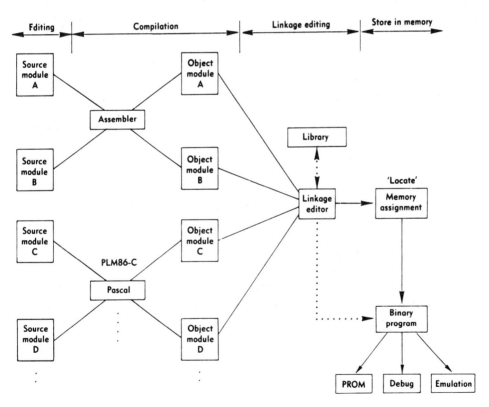

Figure 5.7 The route through the various stages in the generation of an executable program.

157) and is involved in every stage of software testing and software/hardware integration on account of the following facilities which it provides:

- Display of all microprocessor registers.
- Display of memory areas.
- Filling a memory area with a constant.
- Modification of the contents of microprocessor registers or areas of RAM.
- Step-by-step execution of software with display of the register contents after each instruction.
- Introduction and removal of breakpoints in the software; the greater the number of breakpoints, the more flexibility for the user.
- Starting the software from any memory address.

If an error is found, the operator can modify his data or instructions by 'patching' the internal microprocessor registers or the RAM and continuing to search for other possible errors.

All these error corrections must be referred back to the source program and the programmer required to regenerate an executable program (see Fig. 5.7) in order to search for errors again. The search for errors must not be 'are there any errors?' but rather 'how can they be found and rapidly eliminated?'

Note When using the debugger, the user has access only to assembly language (by way of disassembly) or machine language (in the form of ASCII, hexadecimal, octal or binary code). Some manufacturers offer utilities which permit the operator to test software which is written in a high-level language (PLM86/Pascal/FORTRAN), by displaying the software instructions not only in assembler but also in a high-level language.

An example is the Intel 'PSCOPE' utility on the Intellec series III development system or an IBM PC which has 'UDI' software. This overlays MSDOS and simulates the ISIS-II operating system contained in the Intellec and thus enables an IBM PC user to have virtually all the utilities available on an Intellec.

5.4.7 EPROM and PROM Programming Utility

This utility controls the card for programming read only memory. It is available only on development systems in which an EPROM and PROM programmer is incorporated in the system. Programming of read only memories will be described later in this chapter.

5.5 Hardware Elements

The hardware elements consist of the peripherals and a set of cards contained in the development system, the functions of which are indicated in Sections 5.5.1 and 5.5.2.

5.5.1   Basic Peripherals

(a) *The keyboard*
Each system simplifies the calling of standard utilities by a combination of keys. For example, simultaneous pressing of the following pairs of keys:

⟨CTRL⟩ and ⟨H⟩ is equivalent to the HELP command
⟨CTRL⟩ and ⟨E⟩ is equivalent to the EDIT command
⟨CTRL⟩ and ⟨D⟩ is equivalent to the DIR command
⟨CTRL⟩ and ⟨C⟩ is equivalent to the COPY command
etc.

(b) *The screen*
In general these are low-resolution screens which restrict the introduction of software which requires high definition. CAD systems for electronic and mechanical design cannot make use of the most commonly used development systems.

5.5.2   Circuit Cards

The cards which constitute a development system are:

A *mother board* to which cards conforming to the bus configuration of the particular development system are connected. If the project is designed with a bus of the same type as the development system, commissioning of all the cards for the project will be enormously facilitated since any cards designed can be put directly on to the mother board and tested immediately.

Memory boards (dynamic or static RAM); manufacturers offer a wide range of memory capacities within the limit, of course, of the address range of the microprocessors supported by the development system.

A *central emulation unit card and an emulation pod* which contains the emulation card, the buffer module, the interconnecting cable and the connector/adaptor.

This comprises all the most important hardware of a development system; it is used for hardware/software integration (see Fig. 5.8). The connection between the development system and the prototype is achieved by removing the microprocessor from the prototype and inserting in its place the connector at the end of the pod in such a way that the microprocessor of the development system physically and logically replaces the microprocessor in the prototype (see Fig. 5.23). The two microprocessors must be identical. The prototype becomes a target system, all the software is on the development system, the input/output functions of the prototype are activated or de-activated directly from the development system.

The buffer part of the pod serves only to amplify the signals between the application and the development system. The distance between the development system and the prototype is generally around one metre. In a universal development system there are as many emulation pods as microprocessors supported by the system; each microprocessor has its own specific emulation pod.

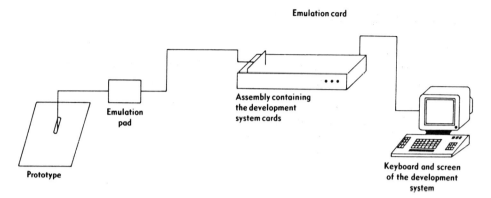

Figure 5.8 The connection between the development system and the prototype.

- *Logic analyser card* with logic analysis pod. This enables a historical record of the states or times during a defined sequence to be obtained; it is generally defined by a breakpoint. This record concerns the information on the three buses of a microcomputer (address, data and control). The display is generally in hexadecimal, octal, binary or mnemonic code.
- *PROM/EPROM programming card.* This loads the executable program into EPROM or PROM. There are two types depending on the development system. Some development systems have an EPROM and PROM programming card which includes sockets (24- and 16-pin) into which the EPROMS and PROMS can be inserted for programming. Other development systems require the purchase of an EPROM programmer independently of the development system; the connection between the EPROM programmer and the development system is generally made with an RS232 link.
- *Parallel and serial interface cards*, for connections to external peripherals such as EPROM programmers, printers etc.
- *User input/output cards.* One part of the card is generally for wire-wrapping and hence for the user to incorporate a specific electronic assembly.
- *Peripheral interface cards*, for the screen, floppy and hard disk units.
- *Wire-wrapping card.* This permits the user to make an electronic assembly by wire-wrapping and test the resulting card directly on the development system.
- *Telephone link for telediagnostics.* Available ports of this type are generally provided with a set of utilities which permit connection to other systems by way of a telephone line (see Fig. 5.30).

Additional possibilities include:

- *Floppy disk unit.* The type of floppy disk varies according to the type of development system; they can be of 3½, 5¼ or 8 inches. The capacity of disks is generally from 360 Kbytes to 1.2 Mbytes.
- *Hard disk drive* (capacity from 10 Mbytes to 84 Mbytes).

Simulation ─────────────────────────────────────

Two approaches to development of a microprocessor based application are possible as follows.

1. *Perform a simulation.* All or part of the functions required of the product are transferred to the development system. Software functions can be realized and tested; hardware functions can be wholly or partially simulated by software; hardware which is complex or time consuming to simulate can be produced on a wire-wrapping board. These boards are available on the majority of development systems and can replace a hardware function which is awaited for the final product.
   The advantages of simulation are as follows:

- Feasibility can be established.
- A microprocessor which is not yet available can be simulated.
- Software developed for the final product can be reused.

The disadvantages are as follows:

- Problems associated with the environment in which the product is required to operate cannot be overcome.
- The time required for simulation must be taken into account when planning the project.
- Mechanical and power supply problems with the product can be neither simulated nor overcome with a simple simulation.
- Execution is generally slower and does not entirely correspond to reality, particularly for projects operating in real time.

2. *Start development, after initial analysis, by producing a hardware prototype and designing the software.* Testing and emulation are then performed as described in the following section.

Note   Simulation is particularly useful when the suitability of a chosen technique is in doubt. A subsequent change during the course of development can thus be avoided.

Testing and Software/Hardware Integration ─────────

5.6   Hardware Testing

A range of electronic hardware tests is suggested in this section; there are other tests and the path described below is given only as an indication; however, it gives good results for the hardware design of a computing project. It is assumed that all electronic devices operate correctly and no individual circuit is defective. Systems for testing electronic packages are not covered in this chapter.

Before tackling the testing of electronic cards in Sections 5.6.1–6, it should be noted that the BASIC language can be used for some electronic card tests; use of this type of language enables time to be saved in the card commissioning process. However, some applications, such as conversion and acquisition of fast data, require a fast response time and the use of a language other than BASIC; it is then necessary to use the assembler or a compiler to produce test programs.

5.6.1   The 'Smoke Test'

Before using a development system, the electronic designer makes a 'smoke test' by removing all integrated circuit packages and then connecting the power. This test permits any short circuits to be located and correct connection of the power to be checked; it is performed for each card used in the project. If the prototype uses a mother board, particular attention should be devoted to it and the power supply points which will be connected to it.

5.6.2   EPROM Tests

One of the values AA in hexadecimal code (10101010 in binary) or 55 in hexadecimal code (01010101 in binary) is loaded into the EPROMs on the card and the contents of the EPROMs are checked using the emulation pod. There are two possible types of error as follows:

Type 1 is associated with the immediate environment of the EPROM. Examples are defective address decoding, problems with EPROM package selection at the chip-select pin, problems with the data or address bus and problems associated with access times.

Type 2 is associated with the card itself. The error is not attributable to type 1; the problem can arise from a poor connection between the emulation pod and the prototype, faulty installation of the three microprocessor buses on the prototype card or a problem with the clock.

5.6.3   RAM Tests

This involves writing the hexadecimal values AA then 55 and reading with checking after each write operation. Errors in this case can arise from chip-select address decoding, the address and/or data buses, the read/write signal (RW), access times and the dynamic memory controller (if one is used).

5.6.4 Peripheral Interface Device Tests

These tests are specific to the various types of interface circuits.

(i) *Programmable parallel input/output interfaces of the PPI and PIA type.*   Program the ports as inputs then as outputs and check for consistency of the physical state of the I/O, measure the voltages and check that the voltage levels correspond to the values required by the peripherals. Program the interrupts and check that they are serviced correctly.

(ii) *Serial input/outputs of the SIO, ACIA, UART, USART etc. type.*   Program the input/outputs and check the consistency of the voltages. Connect the peripheral (console, TTY etc.) and check that the information sent is correctly received by the peripheral (see the following note).

Note   The meanings of the abbreviations are as follow:

SIO: serial input output
ACIA: asynchronous communications interface adaptor.
UART: universal asynchronous receiver transmitter
USART: universal synchronous asynchronous receiver transmitter

(iii) *Programmable timer.*   Program the timer for a number of frequencies and examine the different frequencies on an oscilloscope or with a universal counter.

(iv) *Analogue-to-digital and digital-to-analogue converters.*   Run a data-acquisition program and use an oscilloscope, voltmeter or multimeter on the output or input. Check the consistency of the data and make corrections if necessary (using potentiometers or other passive components). When designing the data-acquisition printed circuit card, it is recommended that potentiometers for

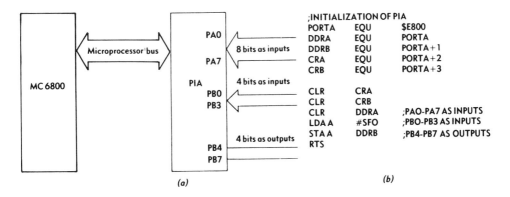

Figure 5.9 (a) The required hardware configuration; (b) initialization software corresponding to configuration (a).

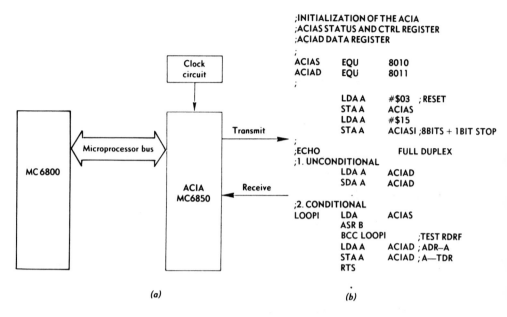

Figure 5.10 (a) The required hardware configuration; (b) initialization software
corresponding to configuration (a).

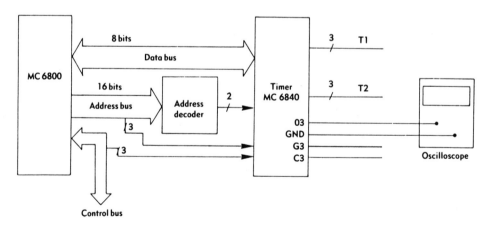

Figure 5.11 The connection of an MC 6840 timer to the bus of an MC 6800.

```
;
;GENERATION OF A PERIOD OF 2 MILLISECONDS ON LINE 03

TIMCR1      EQU       $9000               ;CONTROL REGISTER OF T1
TIMCR2      EQU       $9001               ;CONTROL REGISTER OF T2
TIMCR3      EQU       $9000               ;CONTROL REGISTER OF T3

TIMLR1      EQU       $9002               ;LOADING REGISTER OF T1
TIMLR2      EQU       $9004               ;LOADING REGISTER OF T2
TIMLR3      EQU       $9006               ;LOADING REGISTER OF T3

VALN        EQU       3999                ;FREQ=2*(N+1)*T
;
;
            CLR       TIMCR2              ;ACCESS TO TIMCR3
            LDA A     #SC2                ;MODE 16 BITS, INTERNAL CLOCK
                                          (BUS SIGNAL E)
            STA A     TIMCR3              ;PERIOD OF 2 MILLISECONDS
            LDX       #VALN
            STX       TIMLR3
```

Figure 5.12 An example of a program to test the timer.

correction of analogue voltages should be located where they will be easily accessible during commissioning and maintenance. Possible problems concern the following points:

* Address decoding.
* Access times.
* The read/write signal (R/W).
* Interrupt control.
* Passive circuits associated with converters (resistors and capacitors).
* Offset compensating voltages.

Example 1   The case of an analogue-to-digital or digital-to-analogue converter connected directly to the microprocessor bus.

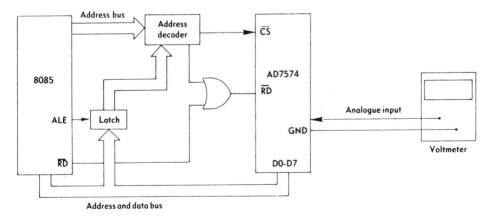

Figure 5.13 An 8-bit analogue-to-digital converter (AD 7574) connected to the bus of an 8085 microprocessor.

```
;TEST OF DATA ACQUISITION LINK
ADRADC        EQU          $9000         ;ADDRESS OF AD7574 CONVERTER

              LDA          ADRADC        ;START CONVERSION
              NOP
              NOP                        ;DELAY=CONVERSION TIME

              LDA          ADRADC        ;READ DATA
```

Figure 5.14 A program to test the analogue-to-digital converter.

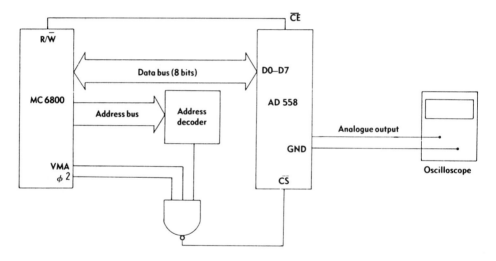

Figure 5.15 An 8-bit digital-to-analogue converter (AD 558) connected to the bus of an MC 6800 microprocessor.

```
;
;TEST OF DATA ACQUISITION LINK
;
ADRDAC        EQU $9006                      ;ADDRESS OF AD558 CONVERTER
;

              LDA A        #SFF              ;OUTPUT OF THE
              STA A        ADRDAC            ;MAXIMUM ANALOGUE VALUE
```

Figure 5.16 A program to test the digital-to-analogue converter.

Example 2 The case of an analogue-to-digital converter connected to a programmable parallel input/output interface (of the PIA or PPI type).

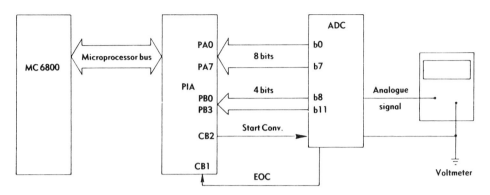

Figure 5.17 A 12-bit analogue-to-digital converter connected to a PIA.

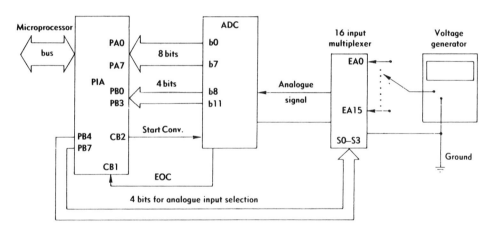

Figure 5.18 A multiplexed 12-bit analogue-to-digital converter connected to a PIA.

(v) Other peripheral interfaces (graphic controllers, floppy or hard disk controllers etc.). The same tests as those cited in (i) and (ii) can be applied (see top of p. 164).

Possible errors for all peripheral interface devices can be due to:

- Address decoding (the decoding circuit, the address bus).
- The data bus.
- The input/output control lines.
- The peripheral interface clock circuit.

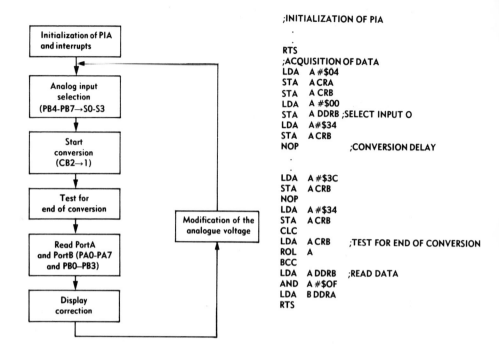

```
                                              ;INITIALIZATION OF PIA
                                                    .
                                                    .
                                              RTS
                                              ;ACQUISITION OF DATA
                                              LDA   A #$04
                                              STA   A CRA
                                              STA   A CRB
                                              LDA   A #$00
                                              STA   A DDRB ;SELECT INPUT O
                                              LDA   A#$34
                                              STA   A CRB
                                              NOP              ;CONVERSION DELAY
                                                    .
                                                    .
                                              LDA   A #$3C
                                              STA   A CRB
                                              NOP
                                              LDA   A #$34
                                              STA   A CRB
                                              CLC
                                              LDA   A CRB      ;TEST FOR END OF CONVERSION
                                              ROL   A
                                              BCC
                                              LDA   A DDRB   ;READ DATA
                                              AND   A #$OF
                                              LDA   B DDRA
                                              RTS
```

In addition to the above tests, each peripheral must have specific tests which correspond to the function which it performs in the product and all the functions contained in the peripheral controller.

The various types of graphics display such as the following should be tested:

- The different types of attribute.
- The different colours.
- The different characters and symbols.

It is also necessary to display a test pattern which enables the correct dimensions of illuminated points on the screen to be checked together with their proper distribution in the display area.

The following tests must be performed on the floppy and hard disk units:

- Track searching.
- Reading from a single sector then from several sectors.
- Positioning of the read/write head.
- Writing and reading the format.
- Reading the cyclic redundancy check (CRC) digits.
- Reading a sector without an address mark.
- Interrupts etc.

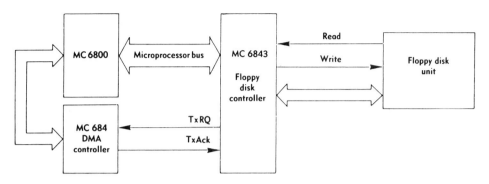

Figure 5.19 Block diagram of the connections to a floppy disk controller.

5.6.5 Global Hardware Testing

Finally, if all the above tests have been performed on each card with positive results, put all the packages on the cards, all the cards on the mother board and test all the hardware.

To test the hardware conveniently, it is necessary to have a range of tests for all the packages in the project. To save time, there should be agreement between the hardware team and the operational and/or firmware team(s).

The start-up, or 'boot', part of the prototype software (see Chapter 3) can be used by the hardware team, since this part of the software includes a complete test of the various electronic packages contained in the product. If, for any reason, this part has not yet been written (it should be written first), similar software must be produced; this same software must be re-used later for maintenance (with the addition of an interactive interface which enables the maintenance technicians to choose the type of test and to observe possible package failures on the screen).

During global testing, in case of error, carefully check the bus drivers on the various cards; the majority of errors arise from these drivers, particularly in respect of data input/output selection signals.

5.6.6 'Burn In' Tests

It is recommended that tests described as 'burn in' should be made; these consist of putting all cards under power for a period of around 24 or 48 hours without connection to the development system. This test enables the reliability of the power supply and the total consumption of the packages to be checked together with all the printed circuit connectors used in the prototype.

This test is performed by loading a simple program into an EPROM (for example, a program to display a message continuously on the console or some other peripheral).

Note   Before leaving this subject, it should be noted that the hardware team may require an extender card in certain cases. This card is necessary when there are mechanical constraints.

Once all the prototype cards are installed in the product, there must be sufficient space for the connector of the emulation pod so that it can be inserted in place of the microprocessor which it is wished to emulate. The extender card solves problems of this type (see Fig. 5.20). This card contains the entire mother board bus and two connectors (one to connect the extender card to the mother board and the other to accept the prototype card where the microprocessor is located).

The extender card can also be used for cards other than that containing the microprocessor, particularly in the case where it is necessary to connect the logic analyser pod to test points on the card which is being tested.

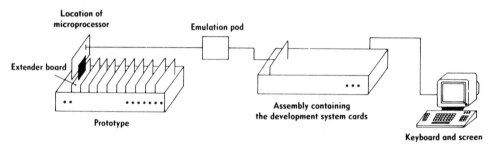

Figure 5.20 Prototype emulation using an extender board.

5.7   Software Tests

The purpose of the three following cases of software testing is to detect the maximum number of software errors (unfortunately some will always remain, which will be a headache for the after-sales service team).

To carry out the three types of test, the following may be used:

- Calls to printer control routines (software entry points to the development system operating system) to print the various values processed by the program under test.
- Calls to system file management routines to create an archive file of all the information which it is wished to check later; these calls are made, in general, after each processing of any value which it is wished to test.

The disadvantage of these two methods is the need for the developer to modify his source software and the procedures to be used to generate an executable program. The result is an increase in the memory space required by the executable program to be tested.

- The debugger; this is the most used tool for software testing. The debugger chosen to provide a description of the contents of this utility is one based on the 8086 microprocessor.

5.7.1   Static Unit Tests

These involve testing each of the procedures of the various modules, by simulating the input/outputs and assigning values to the various parameters of a procedure; these values must be displayed and printed for examination and possible error location. In these tests it is recommended that limiting values (marginal checks) should be taken into account; these limits can be incorporated into the program itself or extreme values can be taken, for example 255 and 00 for a variable of the byte type. The latter type of test enables jamming of the machine to be avoided in the case of errors, which are difficult to locate during subsequent commissioning and can persist when the product is on the market. Errors of this kind are encountered in processing data or a data sequence which has not been anticipated in one or more procedures.

5.7.2   Static Module Tests

This is the same type of test at a higher level of modularity and is also called a static global test. It concerns the functions performed by a group of procedures (see Fig. 5.21) and simulates the data for each function. Each function consists of one or more paths and a path corresponds to the set of procedures called to execute the function. Each function must be tested for each possible case where it may be called; limiting cases (marginal checks) and errors must also be taken into account.

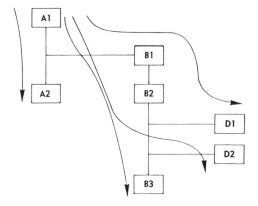

Figure 5.21 Paths representing the various procedures (A1, B1, B2, D1, D2, B3 and A2) called to execute a function in the course of testing. By assigning input values to each function, the operator checks for consistency with the output values. Examples are creation, opening, closure and modification of a file in the case of a set of file management routines.

5.7.3   Semi-dynamic Global Tests

Semi-dynamic global testing is performed when all modules have been tested independently. It involves combining the modules and making global tests in which the hardware is simulated either by software or by access to the hardware available on the development system. These tests include simulation of all possible cases of end use.

These tests are described as semi-dynamic since they correspond to different cases of operation of the product but are independent of the hardware since this is simulated.

It is vital that all tests are repeated after each error is located. It is important that test sequences are as complete as possible so that backward steps are avoided as far as possible. The more rigorous and complete the initial tests, the less the number of errors at the end of the chain, and the errors will certainly be less serious.

Other benefits of this method are the time saved and better relations and communication between the various development teams.

A description of the various commands available in the debugging utility follows:

Initiating and loading the program to be tested

```
=DEBUG
DEBUG 8086   Vx.y
*LOAD   :FO:MODCOM.LOC
*
```

Initiation of the debugging utility by means of the 'DEBUG' command and loading of the executable program 'MODCOM.LOC' to be tested. On loading the program, options can be included of the 'NOSYMBOL' type to avoid loading the symbol table or 'NOLINE' to avoid loading the table of line numbers of the program to be tested; the latter applies particularly to software developed in the Pascal or PLM languages. These two options permit the designer to save memory, which is important when the executable programs are long.

Note   An asterisk precedes the debugging commands which follow.

Execution of the program to be tested

```
*GO
 .
 .
 .
```

The 'GO' command transfers control to the program under test until a breakpoint is encountered, if one exists. Options associated with the 'GO' command are available on almost all development system debuggers; these options are of the following types:

GO FOREVER transfers control to the program under test. Execution of the program can be halted only by an error associated with the development system operating system, activation of the halt key (⟨ESC⟩, ⟨BREAK⟩ or ⟨CANCEL⟩ according to the system) or a program call to an exit routine (of the 'QUIT' or 'EXIT' type).

GO FROM address TILL breakpoint: Execution of the program from the address specified (if it is not indicated the system takes the address contained in CS:IP of the 8086 or the contents of the program counter of 8-bit microprocessors) up to the breakpoint address indicated.

```
*GO FROM 790:0 TILL 481:65C
    .
    .
    .
    .
    .
0481:065CH         PUSH BP
    *
```

Insertion and operation of breakpoints (see Fig. 5.22)

On execution (starting from the 'GO' command), the debugging utility locates the addresses which correspond to the breakpoints and are contained in the breakpoint registers. The contents of these addresses, in the program to be tested, will be saved by the operating system before being replaced by a new value of the software interrupt type (for example 'SWI' SoftWare Interrupt). During execution, each time the program encounters a software interrupt the debugging utility takes charge and restores the former value contained in the address corresponding to the breakpoint of the program under test.

Single step execution

```
*STEP FROM 810:2C
0810:002CH         SBB BYTE PTR[BX] [SI], AL
*STEP
0810:002EH         JE   $+32H
    *
```

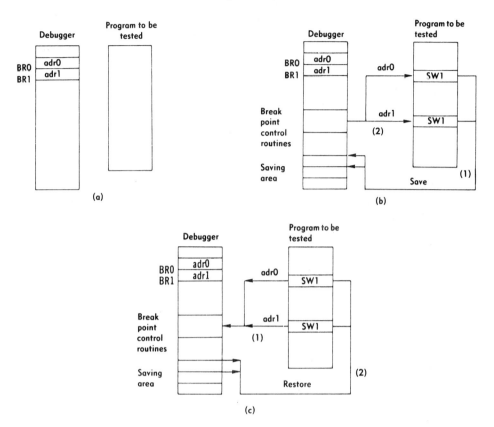

Figure 5.22 Control of breakpoints. (a) Initial state; the breakpoint registers (BR0 and BR1) of the debugger contain the addresses (adr0 and adr1) where it is wished to halt the program to be tested. (b) Initially the debugger saves the contents corresponding to the breakpoints of the program to be tested and loads the software interrupt instruction in place of the values which have been saved. (c) When execution of the program arrives at a breakpoint, the program hands over to the debugging utility which displays the address at which it has halted and restores the instruction initially contained in the program address corresponding to the breakpoint and saved in stage (b).

Each time the 'STEP' command is used, the system executes the following instruction and displays this instruction in disassembled form; the user can examine the various registers and memory areas if he wishes to check for correct execution of each instruction.

Display and modification of the contents of the internal microprocessor registers
To examine the contents of a register, it is merely necessary to type its name followed by carriage return; to modify the contents, the name is followed by an equals sign and the new value.

```
*CS
CS=0481H
*IP
IP=0EF4H
*CS=0400H
*CS,IP,SP
CS=0400H   IP=0EF4H   SP=FEE7H
*REGISTER
RAX=000H   RBX=00BAH   RCX=000 2H  RDX=00A0H   SP=FEE7H
BP=0000H   SI=0110H   DI=0000H   CS=0400H   DS=0F2CH
SS=0000H   ES=0000H   RF=0000H   IP=0EF4H
*STACK 5
W0R   0409:0CDEH=3200H   4330H   3034H   1673H   7560H
*
```

In the same way the contents of the microprocessor stack can be examined.

```
*STACK 5
W0R   0409:0CDEH=3200H   4330H   3034H   1673H   7560H
*
```

Display and modification of the contents of a memory area

```
*BYTE 700:2E
0700:002EH=01EH
*BYTE  700:2E=0FE
*BYTE  700:2E
0700:002EH=0FEH
*BYTE 700:2E   LEN 16=02H
*BYTE 700:2E   LEN 16
0700:002EH    02H    02H
0700:0030H    02H    02H    02H    02H    02H    02H    02H    02H
0700:0038H    02H    02H    02H    02H    02H    02H    02H    02H
*POINTER 700:2EH
POINTER 0700:002EH=1076:0202
*
```

Modification of the contents of address 700:2E together with an area of 16 bytes
starting from address 700:2E and also displaying the contents of the pointer to
address 700:2E.

Display and modification of the contents of ports

```
*PORT D5
PORT 0D5H=20H
*PORT D5=15
*PORT E2='A'
*
```

The value 15 is loaded into the port with address D5 and the character 'A' into the port with address E2.

Disassembly
Disassembly of an address or range of addresses. Disassembly consists of displaying part or all of an executable program (in binary code) in mnemonic form (i.e. assembly language).

```
*ASM 654:8D1
0654:08D1H              LES    BX,DWORD PTR [BP+0AH]
*ASM 654:900    LEN 9
0654:0900H              MOV  SI,0
0654:0903H              CMP   BYTE PTR [S1+03EFH],0
0654:0908H              JZ     A = 03CEH
*
```

Symbol management commands

```
*DEFINE ..MAIN.START = E2 OF BYTE
*
```

The byte symbol 'START' is introduced into the symbol table of the 'MAIN' module; the value E2 is assigned to this new symbol.

```
*REMOVE  .START
*
```

Deletion of the 'START' symbol from the symbol table.

```
*SYMBOL
.TMP=0002.0005H
MODULE..MAIN
.BEGIN=0200:0320H
.VAR=0200:0370H
 .
 .
 .
 *
```

Display of the whole symbol table with the modules which contain the symbols.

```
*MODULE
MODULE   ..MAIN
MODULE   ..MONIT
MODULE   ..LIGNE
MODULE   ..CLAV
 .
 .
 .
 *
```

Display of all modules.

```
*REMOVE MODULE   ..CLAV
 *
```

Deletion of the 'CLAV' module from the symbol table.

Structure of a compound sequence of commands
Some debuggers provide the facility of compounding a number of commands by using a structure enclosed between commands of the following type:

- REPEAT
- COUNT
- IF

A sequence of commands such as those described here is incorporated within this structure.

The REPEAT structure:

Function
The 'REPEAT' structure executes a number of debugger utility commands in the
form of a loop; the end of the loop is determined by the state of a Boolean expression.

Syntax
REPEAT
    Command 1
    Command 2

    .
    .
    .

    Command *n*
    WHILE Boolean expression
    UNTIL Boolean expression
ENDR

Example of use
REPEAT
    GO TILL.CHANGE
    REGISTER
    UNTIL BYTE.VAR = 5
ENDR

In the above example, the program is executed up to the breakpoint 'CHANGE', the
debugger displays the contents of the registers, starts a new execution and provides a
display until the byte 'VAR' becomes equal to 5.

The COUNT structure:

Function
This is the same as the REPEAT structure, except that the COUNT structure makes
a loop counter available which terminates the loop when the counter is equal to zero
even if the condition imposed by the Boolean expression is not satisfied.

Syntax
COUNT arithmetic expression
    Command 1
    Command 2

    .
    .
    .

    Command *n*
    WHILE Boolean expression
    UNTIL Boolean expression
ENDC

An example of use
COUNT 6
  GO TILL.PHIL
  REGISTER
ENDC

In the above example the program is executed up to the breakpoint 'PHIL' and then the contents of the register are displayed; these two operations are executed six times.

The IF structure:

Function
Execution of a debugger command qualified by the state of a Boolean expression.

Syntax
IF Boolean expression THEN command
ENDIF

An example of use
RX = 0
GO TILL.PHIL
IF RX = 23H THEN GO FROM 710:20 TILL.START
ENDIF

In this last example, the register RX is reset to zero, the program is executed up to the breakpoint PHIL, then the register RX is tested; if the value contained in the register is equal to 23H, the debugger will start execution of the program under test, starting from address 0710:0020H, to the breakpoint START.

Exit from the debugger

```
*EXIT
=
```

Exit from the debugger and return to the operating system.
  A debugger such as that described above is generally intended for 8- and 16-bit microprocessors. The arrival of 32-bit microprocessors has required an updating of the debuggers commonly used for 8- and 16-bit microprocessors. This has been achieved by the addition of new functions such as tools for commissioning real-time sections and multitasking systems. Examples are:

- A facility to display a list of tasks and the state of each task.
- The availability, in addition to the entry points listed previously, of another type of breakpoint which could be called a monitoring point or 'watch point' and

operates as follows. The watch point is located at a memory address and each time the contents of this address are modified, the debugger utility displays the old and new values contained in the memory address together with the contents of the internal microprocessor registers.

Greater ease of use would also be much appreciated by system developers.

5.8   Software and Hardware Integration

At this stage, it is assumed that all software and hardware have been thoroughly tested separately and the two parts operate correctly.

The goal of the following stage is to test all the software in its physical environment, that is with the hardware designed for it. The software is, therefore, integrated into the prototype hardware and testing proceeds using the hardware and software tools described below; these consist mainly of the emulation probe and utility.

5.8.1   Insertion of the Emulation Probe

Neither the prototype nor the development system should be under power. The microprocessor is removed from the prototype and the connector at the end of the emulation pod is put in its place (see Fig. 5.23). The location of the connector must observe the pin numbers, pin 1 of the connector must correspond to pin 1 of the microprocessor socket on the prototype card.

Each pod is designed for one type of microprocessor. The function of each pin of the microprocessor must be the same as that of the corresponding pin on the emulation probe. Consequently, in a development system which supports several

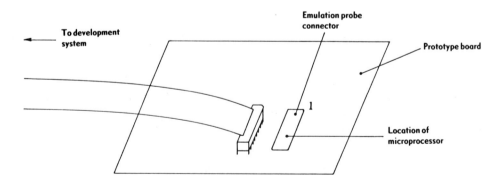

Figure 5.23 Location of the emulation probe on the prototype.

microprocessors (semi-universal or universal), the system must have the option of as many emulation pods as microprocessors which are supported.

The clock can be internal, in which case the development system clock is used. When it is external, the whole system is driven by the clock of the hardware which has been designed. The clock can be selected by hardware (for example in the Motorola EXORCISER, selection is by a switch on the User System Evaluation card (USE)) or by software (for example the INTELLEC).

In some cases (for example the EXORCISER) it is also necessary to select the clock speed and the type of microprocessor from the particular family by means of links (for example MC6800 or MC6802); these selections are made on the emulation card (the USE card in the case of the EXORCISER).

5.8.2   Testing and Emulation (Dynamic Testing)

Emulation consists of loading the program, as it will be in the final product, into the development system. Running this program on the system enables the whole of the prototype to be operated. The designer will find powerful tools in the development system which enable the performance and operation of the whole program to be checked.

Emulation is the most important part of a development system. Although the tools associated with emulation are very similar on all systems, some have greater facilities for particular cases of emulation associated with problems of multitasking and emulating multiprocessor products. So far, emulation of a system with several microprocessors for one application requires an equal number of emulation systems and consequently as many development system stations as there are microprocessors in the prototype. Emulation could be on a microprocessor-by-microprocessor basis but this considerably restricts the most critical part of the test which is interprocessor passing of information and handover of control.

Unfortunately, most if not all development systems are of limited use in multiple microprocessor applications. It is certain that the arrival of 32-bit microprocessors and the development of multiprocessor products, particularly with parallel architecture, will encourage development system manufacturers to offer systems which permit multiprocessor emulation.

Dynamic testing

Using the emulation function, the operator can test the software in its real environment and also detect any hardware errors. Dynamic testing involves the following:

- All functions which are called as a result of operation of the product by the end user; these functions must be tested for all possible cases.
- Interaction between these functions (such as updating of data tables, execution times, synchronization etc.).

- The consistency of messages displayed by the prototype following the various operator actions.
- All hardware input/output signals and the software which drives and processes these signals.
- Interrupts.
- All real-time phenomena; this is difficult since not every possible occurrence and sequence of events can be foreseen.

The range of tools which support dynamic testing must be taken into account from the first stages of development. The general architecture documentation (see Chapter 2) enables the various scenarios to be prepared and the plan of execution (see Chapter 3) permits preparation of the various phases of dynamic testing.

The commands available on an emulator

Initialization
Initialization is achieved by loading the emulation program and selecting the internal or external clock (for some systems this selection is made by links which the user configures directly on the emulation card).

```
=EMUL
*CLOCK=EXTERNAL
*
```

Loading of the emulator and selection of the prototype clock.

Help
Permits display of the set of emulation utility commands together with a message giving the significance of each of these commands.

The 'HELP' command can be called, according to the development system, by typing 'HELP' or simply the '?' character.

Memory configuration
The memory can be defined to be in shared mode (shared by the development system and the prototype), in user mode (the program will be loaded into the memory on the prototype card) or in prohibited access mode (an area which the user does not wish to access).

In general in the case of shared memory, the user can define the areas which are shared between the emulation program itself, the development system resources used by the emulator and the user program. The memory is shared in blocks; the size of a block can vary, according to the development system, from 256 bytes to 8 Kbytes.

```
*MAP 0K  LENGTH 28K = USER
*MAP 28K  LENGTH 32K = GUARDED
*
```

The memory area from 0 to 6FFFH is reserved for the user program and the area from 7000H to 0FF40H is protected from all access.

Loading of the user program into memory

```
*LOAD :F1:MODCOM.LOC
*
```

Loading of the user program MODCOM.LOC (in executable format) into memory in accordance with the memory configuration provided; the program is on unit F1.

Archiving
Permits printing of all the information displayed on the development system screen.

```
*LIST   :LPT:
*
```

All information appearing on the console is immediately sent to the printer.

```
*LIST   :F1:LISTEMUL
*
```

All information appearing on the console is saved in the archive file LISTEMUL of unit F1. This file can be consulted or printed later.

Symbol table display

```
*SYMBOL
.START
.DATAPOR

      .
      .
      .
      .
*
```

This command offers the developer the facility of displaying the contents of the program symbol table; this table is loaded at the same time as the program (the LOAD command).

Defining the code for display of numeric values
This command enables the code for displaying numeric values to be defined.

```
*BASE
H                      ;hexadecimal code selected
*BASE=T           ;Display of digital values will be in octal
*CBYTE 10 TO 30 ;Display of contents of addresses 010H to 030H
0010H=233T   022T   073T   153T   113T   166T   054T   230T
0018H=097T   082T   148T   107T   113T   166T   009T   089T
0020H=134T   062T   101T   077T   166T   233T   022T   073T
0028H=097T   153T   214T   022T   073T   021T   041T   038T
0030H=129T
*
```

'Y' is for binary code, 'T' is for decimal code, 'Q' is for octal code, 'H' is for hexadecimal code and 'ASC' for ASCII code.

Starting emulation
The emulator can be started in a continuous manner (FOREVER) or in a conditional form (TILL).

```
*GO FOREVER
EMULATION BEGUN
```

In the above example, emulation starts and cannot be stopped by any condition except activation of the ESC or END key (depending on the system); these keys are controlled by the development system itself and serve to stop any process unless the whole development system crashes; in this case it is necessary to make a general RESET and reload the program to be tested.

```
*GO FROM  .START TILL  .DATAPORT
EMULATION BEGUN
         .
         .
         .
EMULATION TERMINATED
*
```

Emulation is started from the address where the 'START' label occurs to the address where the DATAPORT label occurs.

The condition can be defined by a label, an address, data, a value of one or more internal microprocessor registers or the state of a Boolean expression.

Single-step emulation
On each execution of an instruction the contents of the internal registers of the microprocessor are displayed (single-step software emulation).

```
*STEP FROM   .START TILL   .CTR>55
         .

RAX=0000H RBX=0000H RCX=0685H RDX=0000H SP=FFFEH BP=0000H
SI=0000H DI=0000H CS=0BE1H DS=0BE1H SS=0BE1H ES=0BE1H
IP=0762H        NV UP DI PL ZR NA PE NC
0BE1:0762  8ED8    MOV    DS,AX

RAX=0000H RBX=0000H RCX=0685H RDX=000H SP=FFFEH BP=0000H
SI=0000H DI=0000H CS=0BE1H DS=0000H SS=0BE1H ES=0BE1H
IP=0767H       NV UP DI PL ZR NA PE NC
0BE1:076B 2E       CS:
0BE1:0768 A30101  MOV [0101],AX

RAX=0001H RBX=0000H RCX=0685H RDX=0000H SP=FFFEH BP=0000H
         .
*        .
```

The syntax of this command is generally of the form: STEP FROM address COUNT *n* TILL conditional expression
where:

FROM address	= start address, loaded into the program counter
COUNT *n*	= number of steps
TILL cond. exp.	= logical expression containing relationships, the conditional expression can be in the form of a variable followed by a relationship (for example, a word, byte, port, register or status indicator followed by relationships of the type =, >, <, >=, <=, <>; numerical expression). For example: TILL.CTR>55.

If the STEP command is used again without COUNT and without a conditional expression, the previous number of steps and conditional expression are taken by default.

Display of the microprocessor bus

Just as single-step emulation described above permits the contents of the micro-processor registers to be displayed after each execution of an instruction, the TRACE command permits the state of the microprocessor bus to be displayed (hardware single-step emulation).

```
*TRACE=FRAME
*PRINT-20
```

FRAME	ADDR	BHE/	STS	QSTS	QDEPTH	DMUX	MARK
0710:	7FFE8H	0	F	S	3	Q	0
0711:	7FFE8H	0	F	N	3	D	0
0712:	0228CH	0	F	N	3	A	0
0713:	683EEH	0	F	N	5	D	0
0714:	50359H	0	R	N	5	A	0
0715:	766FFH	0	R	N	5	D	0
0716:	766FFH	0	R	N	4	Q	0
.							
.							
0729:	7EF77H	0	F	S	5	D	0

```
*
```

The above example enables the state of the 8086 signals to be displayed. The information which contains one state of the microprocessor bus is called a 'frame'. A development system which supports this command can, in general, save around 1023 frames by using the buffer associated with this command, the 'trace buffer', available on such systems. Some systems also have a number of external probes (7 or 8 probes) for signal analysis; these, of course, are independent of the microprocessor signals themselves (that is, the data, address and control bus signals).

Disassembly

This command enables part or all of the user program to be disassembled.

```
*DASM   .START TO .LOOP
        .
        .
OBE1:0100      JMP    0760
OBE1:0103      ADD    BL,BH
OBE1:0105      PUSH   AX
OBE1:0106      PUSH   BX
OBE1:0107      PUSH   CX
OBE1:0108      PUSH   DX
OBE1:0109      PUSH   SI
OBE1:010A      PUSH   DI
OBE1:010B      PUSH   DS
        .
*
```

It enables the user to check modifications to instructions executed by means of the 'ASM' command described below.

Modification of user program instructions
The emulator must enable the user to modify his program.

```
*ASM  ORG  58
0058H
*ASM MOV AL, 05
005AH
*
```

ASM ORG 58 sets the assembly counter on the instruction which it is desired to modify. 'ASM MOV AL, 05' modifies this instruction so that it loads the value 5 into AL.

Enabling and disabling signals and functions
The emulator permits signals and functions to be enabled or disabled either permanently or temporarily.

```
*ENABLE TIMEOUT   ;PROCESSOR TIME OUT SIGNAL ENABLE
*DISABLE TIMEOUT  ;DISABLE TIME OUT SIGNAL
*ENABLE DUMP      ;VALID.ENABLE STEP BY STEP REGISTER DISPLAY
*DISABLE DUMP     ;DISABLE STEP-BY-STEP REGISTER DISPLAY
*ENABLE SY1       ;SYI SIGNAL ENABLE
*
```

Definition and deletion of symbols
The user may define symbols; in the example below, the address FF02H corresponds to the status register of a peripheral interface device and FF04H to a data register of the same interface device. For convenience during testing, the user can assign names to these addresses. The two symbols defined below will be added to the symbol table of the program under test.

```
*DEFINE   .STATUSPORT = 0FF02H
*DEFINE   .DATAPORT = 0FF04H
*
```

Deletion of the symbols LABEL and MOD3 from the symbol table.

```
*REMOVE   .LABEL
*REMOVE   .MOD3
*
```

Display and modification of the contents of internal microprocessor registers
To display the contents of a register it is merely necessary to type its name followed by carriage return; to modify the contents, type the name followed by an equals sign and the new value.

```
*CS
CS=0481H
*IP
IP=0EF4H
*CS=0400H
*CS,IP,SP
CS=0400H IP=0EF4H SP=FEE7H
*REGISTER
RAX=000H RBX=00BAH RCX=0002H RDX=00A0H SP=FEE7H BP=0000H
SI=0110H DI=0000H CS=0400H DS=0F2CH SS=0000H ES=0000H
RF=0000H IP=0EF4H
*STACK 5
WOR 0409:0CDEH=3200H 4330H 3034H 1673H 7560H
*
```

In the same way the contents of the microprocessor STACK can be displayed.

```
*STACK 5
WOR 0409:0CDEH=3200H 4330H 3034H 1673H 7560H
*
```

Display and modification of the contents of input/output ports

```
*PORT D5
PORT 0D5H=20H
*PORT D5=15
*PORT E2='A'
*
```

The value 15 is loaded into the port with address D5 and the character 'A' into the port with address E2.

Modification of the contents of addresses

```
*WORD   .DATAPORT
WOR 0784:0022H=0018H
*WOR 0784:0022H=020H
*
```

The contents of the variable DATAPORT have been modified, the hexadecimal value 20 is loaded into DATAPORT; if BYTE replaces WORD in the command, the contents of a single byte are modified. The internal microprocessor registers can be modified by calling each register followed by the new value.

Structure of a compound sequence of commands
This structure corresponds to that described previously for the debugging utility; it is available, in general, on the majority of emulation systems. It is particularly useful for emulation of real-time software and multiprocessor prototypes, particularly when intermicroprocessor communication is initiated not by hardware (control bus signals) but by a logic state.

Macro-commands
The facility to create macro-commands using the emulator. Examples are as follows:

● Definition of the macro DISPLAY, which displays the contents of the internal microprocessor registers, the port with address E2 and the contents of the memory area from address 030H to 040H each time it is called.

```
DEFINE MACRO DISPLAY
    REGISTER
    PORT 52
    CBYTE 30H TO 40H
ENDM
```

● A call of the DISPLAY macro; it is sufficient to type the name of the macro preceded by the character ':'

```
:DISPLAY
RAX=000H RBX=00BAH RCX=0002H RDX=00A0H SP=FEE7H BP=0000H
SI=0110H DI=0000H CS=0400H DS=0F2CH SS=0000H ES=0000H
RF=0000H IP=0EF4H
PORT 052H=1FH
0030H=0FFH  0D3H  010H  010H  010H  06FH  054H  030H
0038H=09DH  082H  048H  0C7H  0F3H  066H  009H  089H
*
```

Exit from emulation

```
*EXIT
=
```

Exit from emulation and return to the operating system.

Hardware breakpoints

These are similar to software breakpoints as mentioned previously, except that the halt condition depends on electrical signals rather than the logical state of one or more registers.

The number of breakpoints of this type varies according to the development system. The halt conditions can be as follows:

- The contents of an address, by loading the value of an absolute limit or using >= or <= in relation to the value.
- A data or instruction value.
- The state of the read/write signal (R/W).
- The state of signals external to the microprocessor bus (these signals are available, in general, on the emulation pod – see Fig. 5.24).

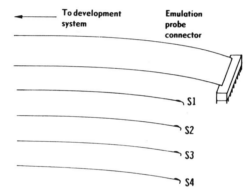

Figure 5.24 The four signals (S1 to S4) which provide hardware breakpoints independently of the microprocessor bus signals.

The halt condition can be a sequence composed of the signals mentioned above and logical operations (such as AND and OR).

Comment Hardware breakpoints can operate in some development systems in 'snapshot' mode in addition to 'halt' mode; the 'snapshot' mode enables the state corresponding to the defined breakpoint to be displayed while continuing processing.

5.8.3   Use of a Logic Analyser

The majority of development systems include a logic analyser system which consists of a logic analyser card and a set of clips connected to a logic analyser probe.

The logic analyser enables the inter-relation of electronic signals throughout the prototype to be displayed. It is particularly effective when timing problems such as delays in initiating and synchronizing electronic devices are encountered; it is also useful for checking the performance and operation of electronic devices and locating spurious triggering due to 'glitches' (distortion of a signal which produces spurious logic levels). The logic analyser must be able to detect and display glitches as short as 3–4 ns.

The power of the logic analyser depends on the degree of interaction with the emulation system; the means available to the operator for locating errors in an efficient manner increase with the extent of interaction. This permits the origin of a 'bug' (software or hardware) to be located, the interaction between software and hardware performance to be evaluated and so on.

In general, the analyser operates by calling up menus which correspond to each configuration or in command mode which permits the user to define the required configuration (see Fig. 5.25).

A logic analyser contains the following:

- Several probes which connect by means of clips to bus test points or device pins (see Fig. 5.26).
- A 'clock' input which is one of a set of input signals and permits the logic analyser and the prototype to operate with the same clock pulses.
- An area of RAM for saving the acquired data; the greater this area, the easier it is to analyse the data.
- A data display in state mode (hexadecimal, octal or binary) or in timing mode (see Fig. 5.28); some logic analysers provide a display facility in mnemonic mode (assembler).
- Two screen area delimiters; these two delimiters permit the user to measure the intervals between two signals or to define an area for enlargement (a microscope effect) to permit closer analysis. These delimiters can be positioned by the cursor keys (left and right) on the development system keyboard (see Fig. 5.28).

The operator can also:

- Program the voltage thresholds at which acquired data are deemed to be valid.
- Program the type of clock (internal – the logic analyser clock, external – the clock of the product under test).
- Program triggering which is associated with defined conditions (the logical operators AND, OR, XOR etc. are available).
- Assign a name to each input which enables the signal to be identified.
- Analyse the data with the help of a set of values or tables. This option is available on some logic analysers and permits unexpected behaviour of the software to be shown up, such as bottlenecks in a monitor.

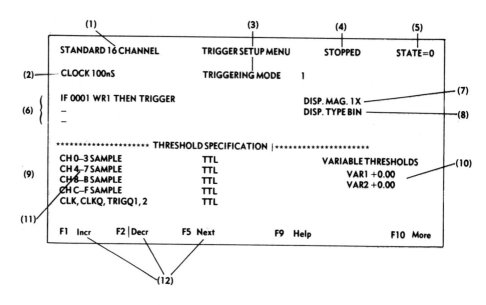

Figure 5.25 Configuration menu of a logic analyser; this is the first menu displayed after power is applied:
1. Number of probes connected to the logic analyser.
2. Statement of the clock speed.
3. Triggering mode.
4. Status message display area.
5. Operational state.
6. Trigger mode programming for the acquisition of data from the probe.
7. Display size.
8. Display type.
9. The channels which correspond to the probe signals and a statement of the type of technology of the signals (TTL, CMOS etc.).
10. Statement of the voltage thresholds.
11. Acquisition mode, by sampling or latching.
12. Commands accessible from the keyboard function keys.

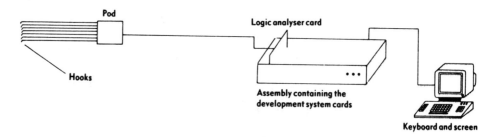

Figure 5.26 Logic analyser system with probes.

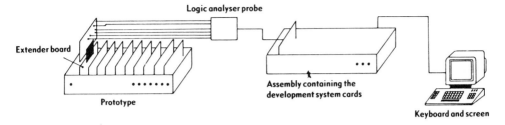

Figure 5.27 Inserting the logic analyser probes into an electronic circuit card.

5.8.4 EPROM Programming

When the tests using emulation are complete and all software and hardware errors
have been located and corrected, the next stage is to load the executable program
into read only memory (EPROM) so that the prototype can operate in 'stand alone'
mode. For this purpose it is necessary to connect the EPROM programmer to the
development system and configure the two systems. Configuration generally reduces
to setting the serial ports of the two systems to the communication characteristics of
the EPROM programmer – the same communication speed (110 to 19 200 baud), the
same parity, the same number of stop bits and the same word length. This is
performed by the serial port configuration utilities of the two systems.

   If the development system does not have an integral read only memory
programmer (EPROMs and PROMs), the programmer is connected as a development system peripheral (see Fig. 5.29). To load an executable program into an
EPROM, the programmer is put into the 'wait' state and then the 'COPY' command
is initiated, for example:

   COPY :F0 :MODCOM.LOC TO :COM :

The executable file MODCOM.LOC contained in unit F0 is loaded into the buffer of
the EPROM programmer, :COM : is the name given to the serial port of the
development system to which the EPROM programmer is connected.

   The following should be checked before purchasing an EPROM programmer:

- Simplicity of use.
- Flexibility in the choice of EPROM and PROM type; it must accept the EPROMs
  used for debugging and ultimately the PROMs used in the product. If PALs or
  PLAs (see Chapter 2) are used in the product, the facilities for programming these
  devices should be checked.
- The capability of covering the various capacities of EPROM (16K, 32K up to
  256K).

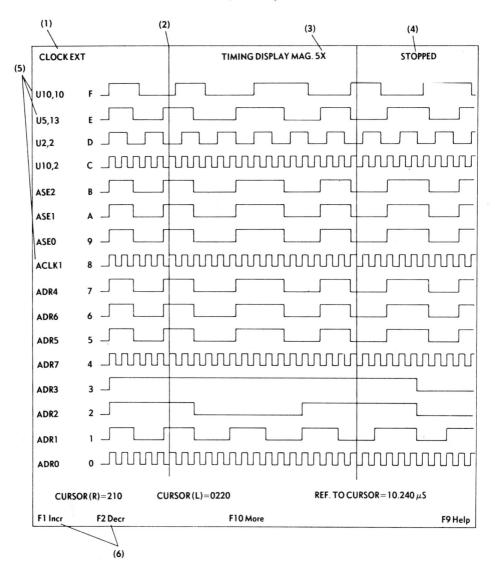

Figure 5.28 Acquisition and display of data in timing mode:

1. Clock type, internal or external.
2. Cursor position.
3. Display amplitude.
4. Status message display area.
5. Signal identification, the listed names are assigned by the user to the 16 probe signals.
6. Commands accessible from the keyboard function keys.

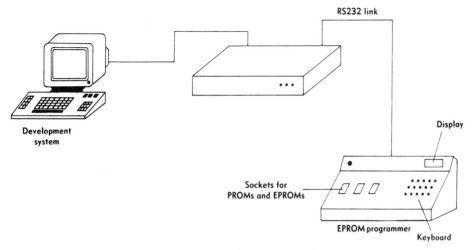

Figure 5.29 EPROM programming.

- The possibility of updating. The supplier should be able to adapt the EPROM/ PROM programmer to future extensions (new EPROMs which are at present unknown) in order to avoid redundant purchases for new projects or later development of the product.
- The available commands are sufficient.

The commands available on EPROM programmers provide the following functions (this list is not complete, there are others):

- Define the EPROM or PROM type to be used.
- Define the communication characteristics of the RS-232 port of the EPROM programmer and display addresses whose contents differ.
- Copy the executable program from the development system into the EPROM buffer and vice versa. This copy must be checked and the checksum or any error displayed; this permits the conformity of the copy to be checked.
- Copy the program contained in the EPROM buffer into the EPROM or PROM and vice versa. The copy must also be checked and the checksum or any error displayed.
- Compare the contents of the EPROM or PROM with the contents of the EPROM programmer buffer.
- Check empty addresses of EPROMs and PROMs and display non-empty addresses.
- Modify the contents of the EPROM programmer buffer.
- Print the contents of EPROMs in ASCII characters.

Some EPROM programmers may have a utility of the BATCH type which enables a string of commands edited by the user to be initiated. These EPROM programmers have a page display for the contents of EPROMs or the EPROM programmer buffer; the display includes the addresses. The contents are in hexadecimal code and ASCII. The latter facility is generally available only on EPROM programmers integrated into the development system.

5.9   Stand-alone Tests

5.9.1   Testing Without a Development System

Testing without a development system consists of testing the prototype in its real environment. The programs are loaded into EPROMs and/or RAMs according to the final use. The tests can start with execution of a number of tasks which the end user can be expected to perform. Some products are required to operate in a particular environment which may pose problems due to noise, large variations in supply voltage, frequent power failures, substantial vibration, critical temperatures and/or pressures, a radioactive environment and so on. The prototype must be subjected to all the environmental tests; it is important to exceed the minimum and maximum environmental characteristics as defined in the project specification by a reasonable amount.

5.9.2   Burn-in Testing

Burn-in testing involves operating the prototype, without connection to the development system of course, for around 48 hours or more in the environment in which it is required to operate. As far as possible all tasks corresponding to final use of the product should be executed.

5.9.3   User Testing

These tests are fundamental for the commercial success of the product. In these tests two worlds are combined – the world of computer specialists and that of users who are not computer specialists.

These tests are all the more important when the final product is intended for non-computer specialists. These tests must be performed by one or more final users. Use of the product by at least three people will considerably increase the effectiveness of the trials.

These trials involve executing all of the following tasks:

- Non-defined tasks: In the first stage the user will attempt to discover, without any documentation, the capabilities of the machine as he may imagine them.
- In the second stage he is required to execute a number of tasks which correspond to the functions for which the machine has been designed.
- In the third stage, the same operations are required but this time with the product user documentation.

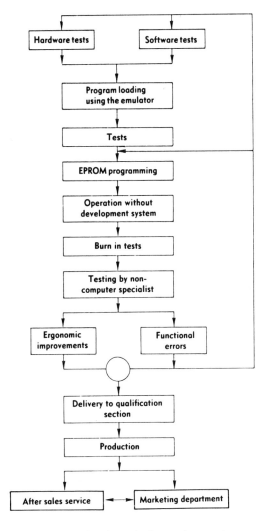

Figure 5.30 The hardware/software integration process.

At each of these stages, users are required to note all cases which seem incomprehensible or difficult. These may relate to displayed messages, the use of commands, the layout of keys or other accessories associated with operation of the product or any other cases, however minor.

The points of operation at which the user questions the operating sequence or the command to be used must be known and are of crucial importance for the survival of the product. If the machine 'crashes' or errors appear, it is useful to know the sequence of operations performed just before the error appeared.

All these factors enable ergonomic problems to be located in the software, hardware and mechanical parts of the product together with any possible operational errors. At this stage, minor errors may still exist in the product but functional and catastrophic errors should not.

5.10   Multiprocessor System Testing

In multiprocessor architectures, the main difficulty is passing parameters between processors via common memory. For this, full testing is necessary and at every instant which processor has access to which memory area must be known in order to locate a defective processor.

Efficient testing generally requires as many development systems as there are microprocessors in the prototype to be tested (see Figs 5.31 and 5.32); operation is slightly complicated when the microprocessors are from different manufacturers (e.g. 80386 and MC68020).

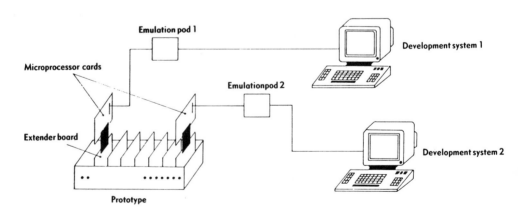

Figure 5.31 Emulation of a dual processor application using two development systems.

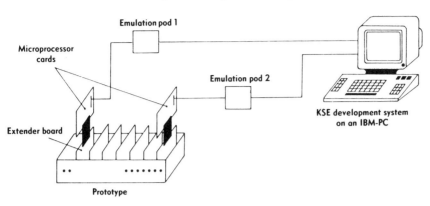

Figure 5.32 Emulation of a dual processor application using a development system
containing two emulation probes (KSE from KRONTRON on an IBM-PC).

To emulate a multiprocessor prototype, the active or inhibited parts of the various
microprocessors should be transferred to the development systems. Interprocessor
dialogue is initiated either by electronic signals (i.e. hardware) or by a logic state (i.e.
software). To test one or the other, proceed as follows:

(a) *The hardware case.*   Use the hardware breakpoints available on the development system to activate or de-activate a microprocessor. These hardware breakpoints must correspond logically to the activation signals of a microprocessor as
designed into the prototype. In cases where these signals do not correspond to
hardware breakpoints, it is necessary to design an electronic circuit to compensate
for this.
(b) *The software case.*   Use a 'compounded sequence of commands'; a loop can be
included in this sequence which continuously tests the logic state which controls
transfer of processing to another microprocessor.

Telediagnostics

When the hardware has been designed, approved by the commissioning section (see
Chapter 3) and manufactured, the development hardware, if available, can be put to
profitable use by the maintenance section to reduce its costs. Telediagnostic
techniques can be used as in the following method:

• If not already in existence, hardware and software are added to the product. The
   hardware is a serial link to be connected to a modem; the software includes a
   communication hardware controller and software to test the various devices and

peripherals (one part of the latter software can be obtained from the product start-up module since the start-up software provides a logical test of all devices).
- If not already available, software is created on the development system which supports telephone communication with the product at the client's site and permits interpretation of the data received from it.
- If several sites are equipped with the same product, the software is designed as a server.
- Significant errors are saved in an archive file and these will serve in the preparation of subsequent versions of the product.

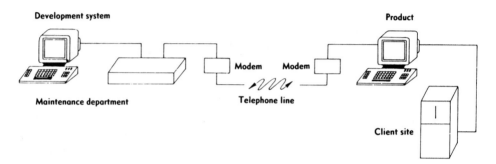

Figure 5.33 Maintenance by telediagnostics using a development system.

Chapter 6

Sustained Planning

6.1   Introduction

Throughout the preceding chapters an attempt has been made to describe the steps which lead to the creation of a new product (see Fig. 6.1). In this chapter, the process will be re-examined from a different point of view. How should the work be managed to ensure completion on time with acceptable quality and costs? Which methods should be used to avoid conflicts and loss of control and to detect these problems sufficiently soon to avoid the consequences? The solution is to provide a management structure which can control planning, evaluation and diagnostics and is acceptable to the development teams.

The evaluation and planning methods to be described in this chapter are intended particularly for medium and large projects which require a large amount of software and/or hardware development and involve interaction between the development teams.

Evaluation and planning are essential to every project. They must be applied with all the necessary rigour and realism. Deviations from estimates can have serious consequences as follows:

- If the times allowed for one part of the work are inadequate, quality is directly affected and 'slippage' of the overall project plan occurs when this part is integrated with other sections of the project. In this context a section can consist of a number of pieces of software (in the form of functions) or electronic hardware (such as an electronic card or power supply).
- If the times are excessive, the cost of the work will become prohibitive (as with a perfect gas which expands to occupy the space provided for it).

Creation of a product is generally the responsibility of a project manager together with those responsible for the development work; if the project is large, one or two people will also be required to take responsibility for planning and this is a continuous operation.

In making use of the resources available, the project manager must:

- Compile a timetable.
- Divide the project into activities.

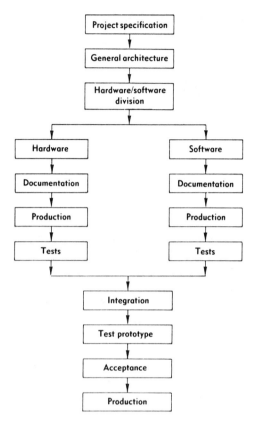

Figure 6.1 Stages in the design of a product.

- List the resources.
- Distribute the activities.
- Follow up the execution of activities.
- Co-ordinate the activities.
- Attempt to maintain cohesion of the personnel involved in the project.
- Lead the teams to the conclusion of the project.

He or she must also:

- Set up a production methodology at all levels (software, hardware and documentation); in particular, for documentation, a clear and precise definition of the contents of each type of documentation must be indicated.
- Check that this methodology is actually accepted and adopted by the personnel.

It is particularly important that those responsible for evaluation and planning should have a sufficient knowledge of computing and electronics (or one of these if two persons are provided). It is also vital that they have the qualities required to obtain the agreement of all those involved. To facilitate the establishment of a favourable climate, those concerned must:

- Be familiar with the problems of group relationships, be aware of the causes of motivation or otherwise of the group and anticipate reactions in order to foresee and avoid conflicts.
- Have good powers of communication as an intermediary between technicians, engineers and management.

The problems associated with 'human sciences' are now systematically studied and are the subject of books, seminars and courses. Topics include group psychology, training in the conduct of meetings, interviewing, communication within a group etc. These topics will not be treated here but their importance should be noted and the reader is reminded of the need to take account of them; the goal is to obtain the co-operation of all those involved in advancing the project and retain confidence until final acceptance.

Some situations which those responsible for the project may encounter, and for which arrangements must be made, are as follows:

- The management may make unrealistic demands of the project timetable. In this case, the person responsible for the timetable, generally the project manager, must:

  * Be able to show the consequences of such demands throughout the project timetable and the problems which would be caused,
  * Arrange periodic meetings between the project manager and the management to evaluate the state of the project and resolve problems associated with delays due to a shortage of resources whether equipment or personnel.

- Several people involved in the project may not know precisely what they should be doing and who is responsible to whom. In this case the project manager must:

  * List all the activities and the steps required to realize them.
  * List the responsibilities and activities of each team taking part in the project.
  * Construct a timing chart showing the stages to be completed up to delivery of the product.
  * Arrange regular meetings with those responsible for each development team to check the state of the project and to correct slippage of planning.

- The project may require regrouping of personnel from different departments, recruitment of new personnel or a contribution from companies which provide services and are external to the organization. These people have different capabilities and may have conflicting views of the project timetable; this must be resolved. The action to be taken in this case is as follows:

  * Check for a clear definition of the terminology used in the project timetable.
  * Check that the methodology is appropriate and that all factors associated with

the identification of activities by codes (which will be detailed later in this chapter) are clearly understood.

* Train personnel having gaps in their knowledge in areas directly associated with the project.
* Train all personnel in the methodology, the terms and the concepts which are or will be used in the documentation, the software and elsewhere.
* Check that the documentation service of the organization is adequately provided with reviews and technical journals which may contain items directly associated with the project.
* Increase the level of participation of those who question the objectives and the techniques adopted.
* Include the time for training, as mentioned above, in the project timetable.
* Once the timetable is defined, avoid all new ideas (except for circumstances which cannot be avoided) in order to avoid changes to the timetable before the project is finished.

• An unavoidable situation may arise in the project which was not originally foreseen. Examples are:

* The need for a component which is later than the date promised by the supplier.
* A change in the situation with respect to competing products.
* Updating of standards by organizations external to the company. These standards may have commercial repercussions on the product and on current products. Those responsible must immediately evaluate the consequences and examine the measures to be taken.

• A certain lack of discipline may be observed with respect to responsibilities:

* Avoid 'short circuiting' the responsibilities of each person at the various levels of responsibility of the project.
* Avoid 'checking up' on activities directly without passing through those responsible for the development teams.
* Be available to those responsible for teams and to the management without having an excessive number of meetings.
* Avoid creating new activities which are not defined in the project timetable.

The project manager must also:

* Communicate with other departments, particularly the research and development department, to locate information such as documents, software, audiovisual information, knowledgeable people and so on which are directly associated with one or more activities of the project.
* Check that members of teams follow the methodology adopted by the organization. If an activity is carried out without following the adopted methodology, this activity must be repeated in whole or in part by the person who performed it while respecting the methodology. In any case the project manager himself should not repeat an activity which is badly performed in any way.

★ The project manager does not need to be familiar with the details of each activity but he does have the responsibility for the consistency of each activity (such as software, hardware and the hardware/software interfaces) and the consistency of each activity with the general architecture of the product. This is the guarantee of homogeneity and global coherence of the product. The time spent on fine detail of one or more activities would be devoted to functions such as:

  ★ Observation of the project timetable.
  ★ Observation of the production methodology.
  ★ Ensuring the coherence of activities.
  ★ Maintaining an atmosphere and spirit of creation.

• At the testing and software/hardware integration stages (see Fig. 6.1) a substantial personnel turnover occurs. Significant delays arise following these departures of personnel since the majority relate to software and hardware technical services.

There can be many reasons for these departures; it can however be observed that:

• Coding (or programming) represents slightly less than 20 per cent of the total development cost, the greatest cost arises in software and hardware testing (debugging) and software/hardware integration (these activities represent around 70 per cent of the development cost). Now, as has been seen, it is at this stage that the greatest effort is needed and the designers of the various sections of the product should be present; in contrast a substantial personnel turnover is helplessly observed. This can be due in part to the fact that the developers have the feeling that:

  ★ They are no longer being creative.
  ★ Their work lacks rigour.
  ★ They are not advancing as quickly as they were at the coding stage and this causes frustration. Unfortunately, these sentiments are often shared by the management and a conflict often arises at this critical stage in the creation of the product. Quite often certain functional problems are located at the software/ hardware integration phase. These require modifications which can, unfortunately, affect the characteristics defined in the project specification. There are many causes of these modifications or 'about turns' such as:

    ★ Poor definition in the project specification due to communication problems.
    ★ Loss of specification documentation due to a flaw in establishing the methodology.
    ★ Inconsistency between software modules or at the software/hardware interface which can be due to communication problems, lack of discipline and/or leadership or general inadequacy of the architecture documentation.
    ★ External intervention which requires one or more functional modifications due to lack of discipline and inadequate leadership.
    ★ Inconsistency of the general architecture which can be due to communication

problems during compilation of the project specification and the general architecture documentation and also to a lack of leadership.

* A difficulty or disparity in the later stages which is difficult to envisage.

This situation has technical consequences which include:

* Modification of part or all of the documentation.
* Modification of hardware and source programs and re-execution of all tests (unit and global).
* Software/hardware integration which involves reperforming all the tests already carried out.

The human consequence is that personnel become completely demoralized, relations between development personnel and subsequently all staff become difficult to establish and to respect.

The solutions are as follows:

* Adoption of a sensitive attitude to personnel from the start; everyone must be aware of this type of problem and particularly the heavy burden of software and hardware debugging and software/hardware integration.
* Preparation of integration tools and test procedures from the start of the project; this should start immediately after realization of the design documentation.
* Motivation of personnel, particularly at this stage of the project.
* Application of a methodology in the design of the various elements of the project and validation of each one of these elements before passing to actual realization in respect of both coding and electronic hardware.
* Establishment of the basis for marketing, the tools for training end users and the requirements for after sales service. These three aspects, in addition to their necessity for successful commercialization of the future product, can be important factors in motivating development personnel.

6.2   Elements of Project Evaluation and Planning

Before examining the requirements for evaluating and planning the project, it is important to recall the conditions under which a project is launched:

* The company management, following the definition of a requirement such as a request, a business plan or an internal requirement, wishes to produce a combination of hardware and software and instructs the technical management to establish or confirm a project specification and to define a provisional overall timescale.
* A project manager is designated whose prime role is to compile an inventory of the resources, both human and equipment, which will be required.

The following paragraphs show how a plan of action will be established and the stages of execution which will be deduced from it and examined.

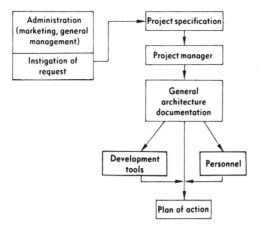

Figure 6.2 The origins of a plan of action.

The project manager has access to information supplied by the management and information contained in the project specification and general architecture documentation. From this he or she compiles an inventory of the personnel and development tools required. These sources of information will serve as a basis for the establishment of a plan of action (see Fig. 6.2).

6.2.1 Harmonizing Completion Times and Resources

During evaluation and planning of the development, several situations can arise which result from the company environment and/or the product itself. Examples are as follows:

- The final delivery date of the product is fixed; the role of planning is to establish the personnel and working tool requirements after the specification has been examined.
- The availability of personnel and working tools is fixed; planning will define the delivery date of the product. The workload is, of course, known.
- The delivery date of the product is fixed and so is the availability of personnel and working tools; evaluation and planning must define two possibilities:

  ★ Firstly, only the availability of personnel is taken into account and the completion date is omitted from the planning operation; the planner suggests a product delivery date in accordance with the availability of personnel and working tools.
  ★ Secondly, only the final delivery date of the product, if known, is taken into account and the requirements for personnel and working tools are estimated.

In the case where the completion date, taking account of the effective availability of personnel and working tools, does not correspond to that defined by the planning operation, the solution must be found by a combined meeting of the planners, the technical and personnel management and possibly the commercial department (particularly if commitments to clients have already been made).

6.2.2   Project Specification and General Architecture Documentation

It is from these two documents, particularly the general architecture documentation (see Chapter 2) that all the elements to be realized can be listed.

It is desirable at this stage that the project manager should hold a 'brainstorming' session with those who will be responsible for the development teams; the maximum number of people should be limited to six or seven. The goal is to establish the elements to be realized and the associated timescale together with the working tools necessary for each activity.

The first phase of the work, starting from the project specification and the general architecture documentation, is to partition the project, by means of a functional analysis, into subsections which will be entrusted to existing or newly created working groups according to the development service structure. This phase is recorded in preliminary documents (subsection functional specifications) which serve as a basis for development.

6.2.3   Human Resources

The list of human resources must take account of the following:

* Availability (date and duration of availability, rate of availability).
* Abilities.
* Holidays.
* For new recruits, the period of integration into the group.
* Training of personnel, permanent and periodic.
* Additional personal delays for unforeseen reasons (illness, family matters, involvement with other products and so on).

The project manager must list the personnel available in the organization and then define the actual requirements of the project; later he or she must produce requests for additional personnel and evaluate the involvement time of each in order to justify recruitment. Alternatively, if this time is short (less than one year), use should be made of service companies.

6.2.4   Development Tools

The project manager must define all the development tools necessary for proper execution of the project up to final acceptance as follows:

- The set of tools necessary for performing the various activities should be listed. This list could be one of the outcomes of the brainstorming session mentioned above.
- The quantity of tools to be distributed among working groups should be defined.
- Provision should be made for maintenance contracts and delays due to maintenance.
- If they are not already in the organization, tools should be made available.

A shortage of tools may be alleviated by the use of other existing hardware in the organization. For example, if development systems are initially unavailable or insufficient, documentation and programming can be started on an available minicomputer provided that the chosen development system has a link which permits importing of files stored on the minicomputer. It is then necessary to distribute the available terminals on the minicomputer among the teams and allocate a time for importing files from the minicomputer to the development system. This importing can be performed as a single batch during the night to avoid monopolizing the terminals. Verification is necessary after importing to detect any incompatibility particularly at character code level.

6.3 Formulation of the Project Plan

All the factors indicated in this section describe the various steps in the evaluation and planning of a project up to its final delivery or 'acceptance'. These steps accompany the running of a project. They are formalized in the documents which together enable all activities to be monitored continuously for delays, excessive costs and the availability of results.

The project plan follows the steps shown in Fig. 6.3; satisfactory execution of each of these steps must be checked, before any publication or archiving, at a meeting between the project manager and those responsible for the development teams.

6.3.1 Project Identification (See Fig. 6.4)

A name and number should be assigned to the project. The number should be agreed with the management, which will use it for its own purposes. This ensures compatibility; the number should remain confidential.

6.3.2 Definition of Activity Identification Codes

The coding suggested below should be adequate; however, each organization may personalize its system but identification methods are generally similar in spite of certain differences in form. Some organizations prefer to put the code 'aa', which

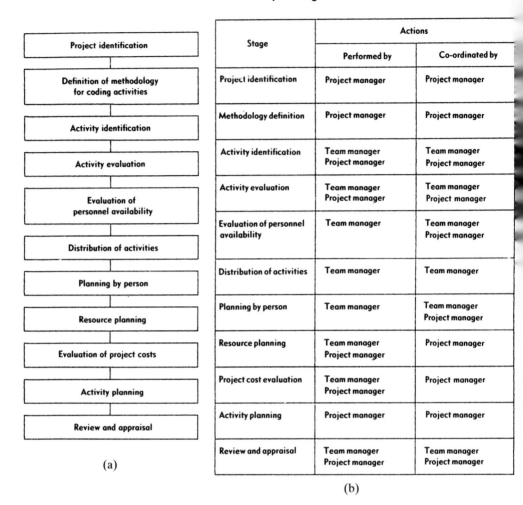

(a)

(b)

Figure 6.3(a) Stages in the design of a project timetable; (b) table of the technical activities associated with each of these stages.

Project name	TX21
Project number	0182-P8

Figure 6.4 Project identification.

identifies the nature of the activity before, the other codes; in this chapter the reverse is used. The project manager determines the choice of these definitions. Each activity must be given a code which is defined as follows:

i	mm	aa	bb

– i   is the identifier for the whole project or sub-project:
0   The whole project,
1 to 9   An activity of one or more sub-projects,

– mm   is the sub-project identifier:
00 to 99 The identifier of each sub-porject and function.

– aa   is the identifer of the nature of the activity:
DO   Documentation, in this case, see identifier 'b' to identify the type of document,
PR   Fabrication of the prototype,
TU   Unit tests,
TG   Global tests,
IN   Integration,
VA   Validation.

– bb   is the identifier of the type of document:
AR   Architecture,
SF   Functional specification,
AN   Organic analysis,
TU   Unit tests,
TG   Global tests,
IN   Integration,
XX   General information.

For example: Activity '1 12 PR' is an activity associated with the 'operating system' sub-project, identified by '1', and the 'software/hardware interface module' function identifed by '12'. This activity is associated with coding of the prototype module indicated by 'PR'.

6.3.3   Activity Identification (See Fig. 6.5)

It is required to identify all activities; to achieve this the following are necessary:

- Partitioning of the project, particularly if it is of medium or large size, into several sub-projects. Each sub-project contains a number of associated functions.
- Identification and listing of each function for each sub-project.

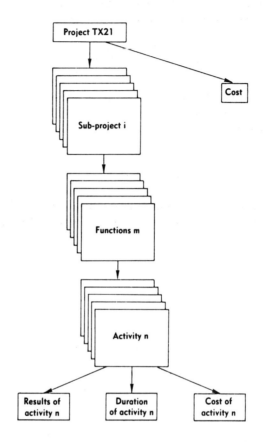

Figure 6.5 Inventory of activities.

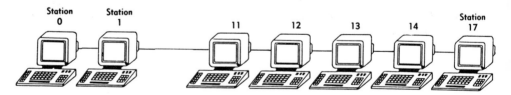

Figure 6.6 Schematic diagram of a group of stations connected to a network.

Identification can be performed by the project manager in conjunction with those responsible for the development teams. The project manager must consolidate the documents concerning all activities. This involves a list of the sub-projects with the names of those responsible for the development teams for each and a list of associated activities. Those responsible for the development teams must consolidate the documents concerning the activities associated with their teams.

Example   Assume that the objective of the project, called TX21, is to produce a product for the general public which supports a range of applications such as word processing and databases, and can have up to 18 terminals in a cluster (see Fig. 6.6). Each terminal can have two floppy disk units or one floppy and one hard disk unit.

Partitioning of this example project separates it into seven sub-projects (see Fig. 6.7) as follows:

*Sub-project 1: The hardware: This contains all the electronics of the product including the central processing unit, memory, peripheral interfaces, floppy and hard disk drives, communication circuits and power supplies.

*Sub-project 2: The operating system: This includes the firmware, the operating system software and the basic utilities; this sub-project is also called the 'kernel' (see Chapter 3).

*Sub-project 3: Communication: This includes all the software for controlling communication and the inter-station links for up to 18 stations.

*Sub-project 4: Applications: This includes all the application software for word processing, the database and so on.

*Sub-project 5: System: This includes additional activities which are necessary for execution of the activities of sub-projects 1 to 4 such as:

- Creation of utilities for transferring files between terminals.
- Preparation of a means of creating executable files.
- Finding and curing 'bugs' or blockages associated with the development tools (such as the use of development system utilities in marginal cases, limitations of workstation memory capacity, 'bugs' inherent in the mode of use and so on).

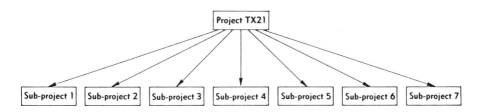

Figure 6.7 Division of Project TX21 into several sub-projects.

*Sub-project 6: Integration and validation: This includes activities associated with the preparation of software tools and standard or special hardware for integration and validation of the prototype. Preparation of these tools must be carried out immediately after production of the functional documentation.

*Sub-project 7: Mechanical: This includes production of the mechanical part of the product. The dimensions of the electronic cards and their location and power supply must be examined with high priority since these are necessary for sub-project 1.

The hardware and application parts, if excessive in terms of workload, can be separated into several sub-projects. However, it is desirable that this separation should reflect the commercial objectives of the project (such as office, scientific or educational use) and distinguish between the functional parts of the hardware. Examples are the central processing unit, the memory (RAM and PROM), peripheral interfaces, floppy and hard disk drives and communication with the input/output processor (IOP).

Example of partitioning of a sub-project

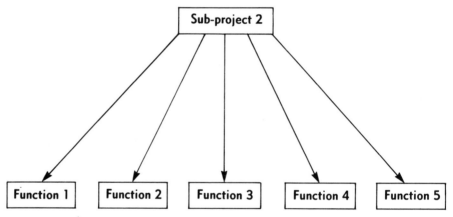

Function 1: Software/hardware interface module.
Function 2: Start-up module.
Function 3: IOP communication control module.
Function 4: File management system module.
Function 5: Peripheral control – keyboard, screen, parallel and serial ports, floppy and hard disk units.

6.3.4 Activity Evaluation (See Table 6.1)

An activity draws together the work required to realize a functional element. The result is realization of hardware, software or documentation. Once all activities of a

Table 6.1 Activity evaluation.

Project name	....	Page .../...	
Project number	....	Sub-project name	....

Author	Responsibility for sub-project	Date:
....	....	../../....

Activity	Code ident.:	Initials of persons in charge
....	....	....

Results of the activity

....
....
....

Start Date ../../....	Finish Date ../../....	Duration ... months	Number of persons	Total work-months	Cost ....

Software: Tools required to perform the activity

....
....

Hardware

....
....

Comments (required documentation)

....
....
....
....

Remarks (interdependence of other activities)

....
....
....
....
....
....

function are identified, a file is established to evaluate the work of each activity; it contains the following:

- The name and number of the project.
- The identification code of the activity.
- The expected results of the activity.
- The number of work-hours required.
- The initials of those in charge of the activity; spaces should be left empty for an external contribution if not already designated.
- The tools necessary for its execution.
- Any information, documents (existing or to be produced) which are necessary for execution of the activity could be listed under this heading.
- The total in work-months.
- The duration.
- The cost, expressed in work-months, for execution of the activity; other costs such as training, travel, attendance at seminars and so on are assigned to the overall cost of the project. All these costs must be consolidated by the project manager.
- Any other comments; interdependent activities should be identified here.

This evaluation is carried out by the development team managers in consultation with the project manager. The file compiled in this way by the team leaders will be consolidated by them and possibly the project manager.

Assuming that the development tools are available, evaluation of the duration of an activity depends on the competence of the person in charge of the activity and his experience of evaluation.

Note   Debugging and hardware/software integration can take up to 70 per cent of the time required to create a new product.

6.3.5   Evaluation of Personnel Availability (See Table 6.2)

Individual files are established for each person assigned to the project. These files can be compiled by the development team leaders and co-ordinated by the project manager and the development team leaders. Each file must contain:

- The person's name.
- The start and finish dates of availability.
- A list of capabilities.
- The number of work-months available for the project; the time required for training, holidays, involvement with other products than the project and so on must be deducted.
- Possible comments.

Table 6.2 A file for evaluating the availability of personnel.

Project name	....	Page .../...
Project number	....	

Author	Name of person evaluated	Date:
....	....	../../....

Availability start date	....
Availability finish date	....
Periods of training/holidays/ involvement with other products/ other absences	....
Number of available work-months	....

Number of years' experience	....

Experience

Software (languages, software debugging tools etc.)

....

....

Hardware (types of hardware, electronics – analog/digital)

....

....

Possible comments

....

....

....

....

....

6.3.6   Activity Distribution (See Table 6.3)

This list which repeats the separation of activities serves to co-ordinate the activities of personnel working in parallel. It should be compiled and co-ordinated by the development team leader, possibly in consultation with the project manager. The list contains the required activities for each sub-project and the initials of persons assigned to each of the activities.

6.3.7   Personnel Planning (See Tables 6.4 and 6.5)

This involves listing all the activities and the time allocated for the projects on which each person will work. The file must include the person's name together with the start and finish dates (and duration) of each activity for which he or she is responsible. The comment section is reserved for identification of activities which are critical because they are interdependent.

Each person taking part in the project must have these two personalized files (Tables 6.4 and 6.5). It is the responsibility of the team to complete, co-ordinate and monitor these files throughout the development period. The project manager can also co-ordinate the information to a certain extent.

6.3.8   Resource Planning (See Table 6.6)

This involves allocating the times at which the development tools will be used. This includes hardware in the form of development workstations, EPROM programmers and erasers, document readers, hardware for testing and so on and software such as compilers, debugging utilities, file transfer and communication utilities and so on. One file for each type of resource is established and should include the period of use (start and finish) and requirements for each period of use.

The team leaders should complete the resource planning files for each sub-project; the project manager must co-ordinate these needs and establish the total requirements for the whole project.

6.3.9   Evaluation of Project Costs (See Fig. 6.8)

If a cost evaluation is made for each activity, each sub-project and the whole project, its evolution can be examined at any time and compared with budgetary provisions both at global (project) level and in the finest detail (which is the cost of an activity). At the global level, the sum of the costs of each activity, such as training, attendance at seminars, travel and others associated with the project must, of course, be included.

Table 6.3 Distribution of activities.

Project name	....	Page ../..	
Project number	....	Sub-project name	....

Author	Responsibility for sub-project	Date:
....	....	../../....

Comments		Initials for action											
....													
....													
....													
....													
List of activities	**Version**												

Table 6.4 Planning by person.

| Project name | | Page ../.. |
| Project number | | |

Author	Person assigned	Date: ../../....

List of activities	Start date	Finish date	Duration	Comments

Table 6.5 Activity planning.

Project name	....	Project number	....	Sub-project name:	Page ./..

Author:	Person assigned:	Date:../../....	From: ././..	To: ././..

Time	Year	Month	Week								
Activities											

Remarks:

Table 6.6   Development tool requirements.

Project name	....	Page .../...
Project number	....	Sub-project name	....

Name of hardware or software: |...

From: ../../....　　　　To: ../../....

No.

12 —
11 —
10 —
9 —
8 —
7 —
6 —
5 —
4 —
3 —
2 —
1 —
0

1 2 3 4 5 6 7 8 9 10 11 12 13 14 15 16 17 18 19 20 21 22 23   T

Remarks:

....
....
....
....
....
....

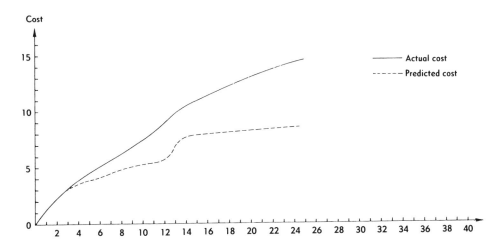

Figure 6.8 Cost-monitoring curve for the project.

In every organization there are rules to guide the project manager in evaluating the cost of the project. The factors taken into account are as follows:

- The duration in work-months.
- The occupation of hardware.
- Training, seminars and travel.
- Involvement of external personnel.

The project manager co-ordinates all information associated with the cost of the project.

6.3.10 Global Activity Planning (See Table 6.7)

This involves assigning times to the various activities in accordance with their duration, the availability of the personnel who will be assigned to them and the interdependence of the activities. This must be done for each sub-project and then for the whole project. This work should be performed and co-ordinated by the project manager who will rely on the support of the various development teams.

Once the planning of the whole project is defined, attention can be devoted to the two following fundamental points:

1. The dependence of almost all sub-project activities on the success of the operating system sub-project. This provides entry points for applications which can make use of any of the product functions. Consequently, completion of the operating system sub-project is fundamental for smooth running of the project. It is the 'kernel'

Table 6.7 Planning the project activities.

Project name	Project number		Date: ../../....	Page: ../..
Author		From: ../../..	To: ../../..	
Time	Year					
	Month					
Activities	Week					
Remarks						

Table 6.8 Choosing between the purchase and hire of a development system.

If	Comment	Decision
PP < PH*P	....	Purchase
PP = PH*P	....	Purchase
PP > PH*P	Evaluate the difference: (PP−(PH*P)) If it is large, − − − − − − − − − − − − −→ If it is not large − − − − − − − − − − −→ (example: PP−(PM*P) = PM*2 months).	Hire purchase

of the whole project in functional terms and in planning its execution. Any slippage of this part will involve slippage of all other sub-projects and consequently the whole project. It will lead to human problems and affect all those involved with the project.

2. At this stage, activity planning allows quantitative requirements for tools and work to be defined exactly. These quantities can vary with time. This can be critical when several production and testing activities arise at the same time. Consequently, it is necessary to foresee and resolve this type of problem either by additional purchases if the duration of these critical periods is long or by hiring if it is short. Taking a development workstation as an example, the ratio of purchase price of the workstation to the cost of hiring the hardware multiplied by the period of hiring will show the best solution (see Table 6.8).

   PP is the purchase price of the development workstation
   PH is the cost of hiring the development workstation
   P is the established period of hiring.

6.4 Monitoring the Execution of Activities

Proper execution of activities must be followed by periodic meetings of the various development team leaders; at these meetings, the activity monitoring files (see Table 6.9) must be reviewed and monitored in order to check that the duration of the activity will be within its limits. All monitoring files should be co-ordinated by the project manager; development team leaders co-ordinate the files associated with their own team.

The various team leaders must draw attention to any slippage and identify any activity which may take longer than the time allocated in order to resolve possible problems by anticipating difficulties as far as possible.

The activity monitoring file must include the following:

- A list of activities.
- The initials of the persons responsible for each activity.
- The start and finish dates of the activity together with its duration in work-months.
- Comments; critical activities must be indicated under this heading.

Table 6.9 Activity monitoring.

List of activities	Initial	Start date	Finish date	Duration	Comments
Project name				Page ../..	
Project number			Sub-project name		
Author		Responsibility for sub-project			Date: ../../....

List of activities	Initial	Start date	Finish date	Duration	Comments

Table 6.10 An activity sheet.

Surname:............ Forename:............ Month:............ Year:............ Assignment:............ Group:............

Project name	1	2	3	4	5	6	7	8	9	10	11	12	13	14	15	16	17	18	19	20	21	22	23	24	25	26	27	28	29	30	31	Days
Training																																	
Unscheduled																																	
Paid leave																																	
Illness/paid absence																																	
Unpaid absence																																	

TOTAL ☐

SIGNATURE:

At these meetings, the development team leaders indicate the following:

- The state of the activities in terms of the time spent and the time required. Any overshoot with respect to the time allocated must be indicated and analysed.
- Problems encountered such as shortage of tools, unavailability of personnel (scc Table 6.10), awaited delivery of modules on which other activities depend and so on.

The minutes of these meetings (see Table 6.11) should be circulated to all personnel taking part in the project.

The project manager has the following responsibilities:

- Informing the management of the state of advancement of the project.
- Resolving problems of resource shortages (personnel and/or development tools).
- Monitoring the coherence of activities.
- Resolving communication problems if they exist.
- Ensuring correct financial management of the budget allocated to the project and, in co-ordination with the development team leaders, monitoring the costs of activities.
- Making corrections, if necessary, to achieve the defined objectives by a planning modification, adaptation of the organization and so on.

6.5 Project Conclusion

Before arriving at the final acceptance itself, care should have been taken, in parallel with the technical development of the product, to prepare the sales and after-sales service support.

These actions make an important contribution to the success of the product. Their establishment, even before the appearance of the first prototypes, improves the motivation of the personnel developing the product and increases the possibility of commercial success of the product.

The following should be made available in good time:

- Commercial documentation which must be compiled by the commercial department. In addition to its activities on all commercial aspects, the commercial department, through its constant interface with end users of products, can have a determining influence on the product by considering all aspects which are visible to the end user of the product. This advice relates both to the user documentation and the ergonomic aspects. Comments of this type on the characteristics of the product, preferably at the start of development, enable their repercussion on costs to be examined in time.

  These exchanges with the technical department also permit the commercial department to become familiar with the product and hence facilitate relations with future users.
- Product user documentation, which is generally addressed to non-computer

Table 6.11   Minutes of a meeting.

Project name	....	Project number	....	Page ../..

Held on: ../../..	A:.........................	Drafted: ../../..	By:...............................

Participants:	Circulation:
....	....
....	....
....	....
....	....
....	....

Objective:...

Report of proceedings:	Actions/conclusions
....	
....	
....	
....	
....	
....	
....	
....	
....	
....	
....	
....	
....	
....	
....	
....	
....	
....	
....	
....	
....	
....	
....	
....	
....	

specialists (see Chapter 3). Checking of this documentation must be done by the commercial department.

- Program documentation, intended for developers of applications of the new product (see Chapter 3). This describes all the entry points to the system and product utilities and includes the names of procedures and parameters, their type, their significance and an example of use.
- Support for user-training seminars. This support includes documentation, audio-visual aids and others. With the help of this support, internal training seminars for sales people can be initiated; comments and criticisms at this stage enable the support to be improved.
- The tools necessary for the qualification department. The product development department must make all the necessary information available to the qualification department, particularly the list of tests which have been performed throughout the development period.
- The tools necessary for after-sales service. After detailed training on the component parts of the product, this service team must prepare the tools which will be necessary for customer service and telediagnostics, if used. These tools can be of many types such as logic analysers, development systems, oscilloscopes, multimeters, maintenance documentation and files which record and archive breakdowns.

Before delivery of any prototype, internal checking by the development team should be carried out. This checking is carried out in accordance with the conditions defined in the project specification; it must include all the documentation required by other services.

The end of a project is formalized by an acceptance test whose content is, in general, defined in the project specification. This acceptance test depends on conditions established at the start of the project:

- In the case of sub-contract work, the final acceptance test generally includes all the elements produced in accordance with the contract between the organizations which are signatories to it.
- In the case of the organization's own product, the development department must hand over to the test department in the majority of cases. The items included in the acceptance test include the following:

  ★ The actual number of prototypes (3–10 prototypes).
  ★ All the source software.
  ★ All the executable files.
  ★ Executable file generation utilities, generally in the form of batch files.
  ★ The list of utilities necessary for controlling the system and applications.
  ★ Documentation (software, hardware and mechanical).
  ★ Other information such as the types of test and associated results.

The acceptance test is carried out by the receiving section of the organization which initiated the tender. When the product was requested by the company which has developed it in order to market it, there is no acceptance test as such. The product is then received by a 'qualification service' whose role is to take the place of end users and consider all conditions of use which could arise and to check for correct operation of the product for each of these conditions. The qualification service is often associated hierarchically with the commercial and marketing departments since it must be quite independent of the development department.

The project is not finished after the acceptance test as defined above since the following must be produced after delivery:

- A manufacturing dossier which must be updated to permit production of the new product to be initiated by the project and production managers.
- A dossier for the after-sales service to perform software and hardware maintenance on site or by telediagnostics. This should be compiled by the project manager and the after-sales service manager.
- A dossier for the department which trains users of the new product. It is important to identify the true end user for all applications of the product. This should be compiled by the project manager and the training service manager.

The commercial department has already been involved for some time, certainly before the production phase, but in the last resort it is this department which will have to overcome difficulties which can arise with the first customers and which will require solutions from the development department. This is why in some cases, where the product is intended for series production, one or more 'pilot customers' are asked to be the first users. Each pilot customer is monitored for a certain time by the commercial department and one or more persons designated by the development department. The definitive production dossier is finalized only after the result of this pilot-customer-monitoring phase.

Bibliography

Books

Aumiaux M., *Les systèmes à microprocesseurs* (2nd edn), Masson: Paris, 1982.

Ball R. and Pratt R., *Engineering Applications of Microcomputers*, Prentice Hall: Hemel Hempstead, 1986.

Bellino J., Bétourné C., Briat J., Canet B., Cleemann E., Derniame J.-C., Ferrié J., Kaiser C., Krakowiak S., Mossière J. and Verjus J.-P., *Systèmes d'exploitation des ordinateurs*. Dunod Université, Paris, 1975.

Ginguay M. and Lauret A., *Dictionnaire d'informatique* (3rd edn), Masson, Paris, 1987.

Jensen K. and Wirth N., *PASCAL manuel de l'utilisateur* (4th edn), Eyrolles, 1983.

Meinadier J. P., *Structure et fonctionnement des ordinateurs*, Larousse, 1971.

Meyer B. and Baudoin C., *Méthodes de programmation* (2nd edn), Eyrolles, 1980.

Sheingold D. H., *Nonlinear circuits handbook* (2nd edn), Analog Devices, Inc., 1976.

CHMOS Components Handbook, Intel Corporation, 1985.

Data-acquisition Data Book 1984, Volumes I and II, Analog Devices, Inc., 1984.

Development Systems Handbook, Intel Corporation, January, 1985.

Linear Interface Integrated Circuits, Motorola Inc., 1980.

Manuel de démonstration iPDS, Intel Corporation.

Memory Components Handbook, Intel Corporation, 1985.

Microcomputer Components, Motorola Inc., 1979.

Reference manual – Transputer architecture. INMOS Limited, October, 1986.

The European CMOS Selection, Motorola Inc., 1979.

Articles

Allison A., 'RISCs challenge mini, micro suppliers', *Mini-Micro Systems*, 127–136, November, 1986.

Anh-No M., 'L'accès direct à la mémoire', *Micro-Systèmes*, 47–51, July–August, 1981.

Beresford R., Evanczuk S. and Suydam W. E., 'Flat-panel displays flash a message to industry's eyes', *Electronics*, 125–129, 5 May, 1982.

Blanchard M., 'Définition d'un système de développement: premiers éléments de choix', *Minis et Micros*, 48–52, No. 177.

Böhm C. and Jacopini G., *Flow Diagrams, Turing Machines and Languages with only Two Formation Rules*, ACM9 No. 3, May, 1966.

Breuninger R. K., 'Control static-column DRAM with improved logic array', *Electronic Design*, 91–95, 9 July, 1987.

Brown P. M., 'High-speed video DACs drive CRTs to new performance heights', *EDN*, 201–208, 3 September, 1987.

Bursky D., 'Subnanosecond silicon ECL gate arrays face challenge from GaAs and CMOS', *Electronic Design*, 74–84, 12 June, 1986.

Cloke B., 'Run-length-limited coding increases disk-drive capacity', *EDN*, 199–202, 21 March, 1987.

Cole B. C., 'The exploding role of nonvolatile memory', *Electronics*, 47–56, 21 August, 1986.

Cole B. C., 'How a cache control chip supercharges 386 processor', *Electronics*, 74–76, 11 June, 1987.

Cole B. C., 'Programmable logic devices: faster, denser, and a lot more of them', *Electronics*, 61–72, 17 September, 1987.

Collins K. N., 'Single-chip interface eases data separator design in harddisk control circuits', *Electronic Design*, 145–148, 6 March, 1986.

Connolly E., 'Computer Standards. Designer's Reference', *Electronic Design*, 117–131, 23 December, 1982.

Cruess M. W., 'Memory management chip for 68020 translates addresses in less than a clock cycle', *Electronic Design*, 151–161, 15 May, 1986.

Dijkstra E. W., *Notes on Structured Programming*, Technische Hogeschool, Eindhoven: Netherlands, 1970.

Doris A., 'Les principes de la visualisation', *Micro-Systèmes*, 47–54, July–August, 1979.

Duquesne J. L., 'Analyse logique: la troisième génération', *Électronique Industrielle*, 133–138, No. 31, 1 April, 1982.

Eckert K., 'A multiprocessor interface', *IEEE MICRO*, 67–70, November, 1982.

EDN Staff., 'Defensive programming simplifies program maintenance', *EDN*, 157–160, 7 August, 1986.

Evanczuk S., 'Real-time OS', *Electronics*, 105–115, 24 March, 1983.

Freeman E., 'Printed-circuit-board design service bureaus', *EDN*, 126–138, 8 August, 1985.

Freeman E., 'Software packages for standard 32-bit CAE/CAD workstations', *EDN*, 134–142, 26 June, 1986.

Friedman, M. G. W., 'In-house IC design reduces costs and increases control', *EDN*, 265–269, 18 April, 1985.

Gross, C. 'Un renouveau en conception des circuits imprimés', *Électronique Industrielle*, 102–109, No. 93, 15 September, 1985.

Guillemaud P., 'CAO: intégration de la conception jusqu'au testeur', *Électronique Industrielle*, 73–78, No. 83, 15 February, 1985.

Haight J., 'GaAs logic characteristics result in integration problems', *EDN*, 225–232, 28 June, 1984.

Hayes, N., 'Specifying multilayer circuit boards to meet the demands of VLSI', *Electronics*, 157–161, 10 February, 1983.

Hemenway J., 'Extend μC capability via multiprocessing', *EDN*, 175–180, 14 April, 1982.

Hemenway J., 'Virtual-kernel design makes multiprocessing go', *EDN*, 215–220, 1 September, 1982.

Hornstein J. V., 'Parallel processing attacks real-time world', *Mini-Micro Systems*, 65–77, December, 1986.

Hugelshofer W. and Schultz B., 'Cache buffer for disk accelerates minicomputer performance', *Electronics*, 155–159, 10 February, 1982.

Johnson B., 'Smart link interfaces computer and peripherals', *Electronics*, 119–124, 11 August, 1982.

Juliff M. F., 'Testing Winchester disk drives', *Mini-Micro Systems*, 239–242, February, 1983.

Keely W. A., 'Knowledge of documentation eases military design tasks', *EDN*, 181–192, 23 August, 1984.

Kumar V. S. 'Consider static-RAM cache memory for 32-bit μC design', *EDN*, 187–192, 11 June, 1987.

Lagrange G., 'Entre analyseurs logiques et systèmes, rupture ou convergence?', *Électronique Industrielle*, 56–64, No. 67, 15 March, 1984.

Lassen C. L., 'Wanted: a new interconnection technology', *Electronics*, 113–121, 27 September, 1979.

Leibson S. H., 'Project-management software for PCs helps you map out a plan for your project', *EDN*, 57–64, 5 February, 1987.

McDermott J., 'Industrial Interconnect Devices', *EDN*, 129–142, 9 August, 1987.

Manuel T., 'Molting computer terminals to human needs', *Electronics*, 97–108, 30 June, 1982.

Mears J., 'To clear system bottlenecks drive backplanes with ECL', *Electronic Design*, 83–88, 15 October, 1987.

Mokhoff N., 'Videopalette raises color ante to 1024 separate hues', *Electronic Design*, 43–46, 20 August, 1987.

Montois J.-J., 'Les mémoires à semi-conducteurs: I – Les dispositifs à lecture seule', *Micro-Systèmes*, 45–60, July–August, 1982.

Montois J.-J., 'Les mémoires à semi-conducteurs: II – Les dispositifs à lecture/écriture', *Micro-Systèmes*, 81–95, September–October, 1982.

Nalesnik R., 'Cache accelerates operation of 32-bit μP systems', *EDN*, 183–188, 28 May, 1987.

Noël S., 'Supports magnétiques: les modes d'encodage et leurs conséquences pratiques', *Minis et Micros*, 25–31, No. 132, 19 .

Ormond T., 'Dedicated prototype panels simplify bus interfacing tasks', *EDN*, 194–201, 9 July, 1987.

Overgaard M., 'Bring greater portability to application programs', *Electronics*, 135–140, 11 August, 1982.

Pantano G., 'Simulation: de la conception au test', *Électronique Industrielle*, 59–63, No. 95, 15 October, 1985.

Patton C., 'Software opens the way to true concurrency for multiprocessing', *Electronic Design*, 83–90, 8 August, 1985.

Price S. M., 'CMOS 256-kbit video RAM, with wide two-way bus, picks up speed, drops power', *Electronic Design*, 171–177, 19 September, 1985.

Ramsay M. and Shaffer T. A., 'Custom video control delivers advanced font graphics', *Electronics*, 151–154, 15 December, 1981.

Rice V., 'Specific memories: A $1billion business by 1991', *Electronic Business*, 88–89, 15 June, 1987.

Richardson B., 'Microprogram monitor helps develop bit-slice designs', *EDN*, 191–196, 31 March, 1987.

Ricouard J. P., 'Pour le développement d'applications à microprocesseurs: de la station monoposte au système multipostes', *Électronique Industrielle*, 43–45, No. 39, 1 October, 1982.

Rockmore A. J., 'Knowledge-based software turns specifications into efficient programs', *Electronic Design*, 105–112, 25 July, 1985.

Rowe P. L. 'Bootstrap firmware simplifies CPU programming', *EDN*, 171–180, 20 February, 1986.

Segal M., 'Disk-controller IC varies SCSI bus interface designs', *EDN*, 215–222, 16 May, 1985.

Seymour P., 'Circuit de gestion mémoire: organisation de la 68451', *Minis et Micros*, 39–45, No. 144.

Shear D., 'Cache-memory systems benefit from on-chip solutions', *EDN*, 245–260, 10 December, 1987.

Simpson D., 'How to choose the best CAD platform', *Mini-Micro Systems*, 67–87, July, 1987.

Small C. H., 'Development systems for 32-bits μPs', *EDN*, 107–122, 13 June, 1985.

Small C. H., 'Software debuggers struggle to meet engineer's needs', *EDN*, 143–150, 12 December, 1985.

Tellier J. and Bell D., 'Single-chip, 2-port RAM controller saves board space', *EDN*, 165–170, 23 January, 1986.

Thomsen G., 'Disk controller supports both rigid and floppy drives', *EDN*, 165–174, 4 October, 1984.

Tyler J. E. M., 'Extending microprocessor emulators', *Electronic Engineering*, 56–58, February, 1983.

Warner C. W., 'Combine C and assembly language for the 8086/88', *EDN*, 195–198, 18 March, 1987.

Wright M., 'μP simulators let you debug software on an IBM-PC', *EDN*, 196–204, 11 December, 1986.

Wright M., 'High-speed EPROMS', *EDN*, 133–138, 17 September, 1987.

Zuhl M., 'Coprocessing expedites software-hardware development', *Electronics*, 122–126, 30 June, 1982.

Index